*MURDEROUS MATHS

THE ESSENTIAL ARITHMETRICKS

How to + - × ÷

KJARTAN POSKITT

Illustrated by
Daniel Postgate

Hippo

With many thanks to Tracy Turner at Scholastic.
This is the tenth book we've worked on together
and it's been fun all the way.

Scholastic Children's Books,
Euston House, 24 Eversholt Street,
London, NW1 1DB, UK
A division of Scholastic Ltd
London ~ New York ~ Toronto ~ Sydney ~ Auckland
Mexico City ~ New Delhi ~ Hong Kong

Published by Scholastic Ltd, 1999

10 digit ISBN 0 439 01157 4
13 digit ISBN 978 0439 01157 0

Typeset by TM Typesetting, Midsomer Norton
Printed and bound in Denmark by Nørhaven Paperback A/S, Viborg

13 15 17 19 20 18 16 14

CONTENTS

.MURDEROUS MATHS.

JOIN THE MURDEROUS MATHS GANG
FOR MORE FUN, GAMES AND TIPS AT
www.murderousmaths.co.uk

Also by Kjartan Poskitt:
The Knowledge: The Gobsmacking Galaxy
Dead Famous: Isaac Newton and his Apple

WHAT ARE THE ESSENTIAL ARITHMETRICKS?

Everybody can be utterly brilliant at something, but it doesn't matter whether it's conjuring, cooking, carpentry or even kissing, you have to start at the bottom and get to grips with the bare essentials.

In maths the bare essentials – adding, subtracting, multiplying and dividing – are called "arithmetic". Once you've got the hang of the basic tricks involved in doing them, then you'll be on your way to designing your own space rocket, building up a fabulous business empire and having your own skyscraper, or even inventing an amazing new number that nobody else has ever thought of. Wahey! But before we dive in let's see how important a few essential tricks are to a completely different subject – painting.

Suppose you wanted to buy *Sunflowers* by the Dutch artist Vincent Van Gogh, you would have to wave goodbye to at least £25 million and probably a lot more! That's not bad for one oil painting is it? But did Vincent start out

5

doing really top range pictures like that? No of course he didn't. Like everybody else, he had to start at the bottom and learn the essential tricks.

First of all he needed to get the hang of important details such as...

- A brush won't make a mark unless you put some paint on it first.
- It's easier to keep the paper still and move the brush about rather than the other way round.

Next he had to learn more complicated stuff like this...

- If you're painting the countryside, the sky should be blue and go along the top, and the grass should be green and go along the bottom.
- Trees are bigger than flowers, unless they are a lot further away in which case they are still bigger but look smaller.
- People have two eyes with a nose in the middle. (Funnily enough Pablo Picasso never learnt this one, but his pictures still go for the same sort of money as Vincent's.)

Here are some of Vincent's very first pictures:

Of course, this was just a start but without it

6

Vincent would never have got so good. Who knows? If he'd kept at it, he might have been talented enough to do the pictures for a *Murderous Maths* book.

With maths it's just the same. We have to start by learning to count 1-2-3, next we move on to adding and multiplying and generally squidging numbers about, then gradually we build up to the good stuff.

Now we need an idiot to write in with a stupid question.

Dear murderous Maths
Why have we got to learn
adding and multiplying and
generally squidging numbers
about when there are computers
and calculators to do it for us?
Yours Thickly
Annie Jott.

Well, suppose Van Gogh had said:

I CAN'T BE BOTHERED WITH PAINTING. I'll TAKE A PHOTO INSTEAD.

Nobody would be paying umpteen millions just for a snapshot of a few flowers would they?

So much for the art world. This book is going to introduce you to a completely different world full of exploration, discovery, fun, games, challenges, tricks and triumphs, and probably most important of all – money!

Whether you become a sports star, an artist, a pop singer or the prime minister – at some point you are going to wonder if you've been given the right wages, and when it comes to working it out the best person to trust is yourself, providing you know some murderous maths.

So what are you waiting for?

Sure, you can try and sneak by with fudged answers or getting help from a sweaty little electronic box, but sooner or later you'll show yourself up. The only way to really survive and go on to be a champion is to get your head around ... **THE ESSENTIAL ARITHMETRICKS.**

BACK TO THE SANDPIT

Weren't lessons absolutely brilliant when you first started school? Instead of French, History, Maths, Science or any of those things – you got lessons like sandpit, storytime and building-blocks. Isn't it a pity you can't keep doing sandpit, and when you leave school you could even do sandpit exams?

What you probably didn't realize though is that murderous maths gets everywhere, it even sneaks into "sandpit". Look at this:

This might seem innocent enough, providing you know what "3" means. Of course you're thinking that everybody must know what "3" means – but believe it or not there are some people who cannot decide.

Pure mathematicians – brilliant or barking?
As you probably know, scientists have found out that everything is made up of tiny atoms. Even if they invent the smartest computer or build the coolest car, they can't help using atoms because that's all they've got. Consequently atoms are very interesting to scientists and they spend a lot of time studying them to see what they are made of, and

9

even wondering how they got to be there in the first place. They even wonder WHY atoms got to be there in the first place. Did the atoms actually choose to exist? Or did someone tell them to?

OI YOU! START EXISTING!

It's amazing the weird things that scientists worry about, isn't it?

Mathematicians are just as bad. They can invent awesome formulas or calculate the movements of planets and stars, but whatever they do, they can't help using numbers. In the same way that scientists worry about what atoms are, there are people called "pure" mathematicians who worry about what numbers are. These can be quite normal looking people who get up, eat their cornflakes, catch the bus to work, then sit in an office all day just wondering "what is 3?"

Anyway, let's get back to the sandpit. There you were in your little pink bloomers toddling up to have a turn, but as you got there you realized there were three people already in it. How did you manage to do that? Because unlike some pure mathematicians, you knew what "3" was, even if you did have a bit of dribble going down your chin. Incredible as it may seem, you had already mastered your first bit of Murderous Maths.

Sadly something unfair has just happened. Four more kids have decided to break the rules and push past you into the sandpit to join the three kids already there. How can you work out the number of kids in the sandpit all together? There are two methods...

● You could count them all and get to seven like this: 1, 2, 3, 4, 5, 6, 7.
● You could start counting from three, and count up one number for each extra kid that has joined in: 4, 5, 6, 7.

You might not see much difference in these two methods, but it becomes more obvious with bigger numbers.

Suppose you have 35 kids already in the sandpit, and four more come in. How can you work out how many kids are in the sandpit?

● You could count all 39 of them: 1, 2, 3, 4, 5, 6, 7... yawn snore bump ouch! Where had we got to?
● You could start at 35 and count up one number for each extra kid that comes in: 36, 37, 38, 39.

So which do you think is easier?

Here's the clever bit. When you first learnt to count, you just learnt to say the numbers in order. One, two, three and so on. You then went on practising your counting up to higher and higher numbers, and that's how you know how to count. OR IS IT?

Let's take one more trip back to the sandpit and you're so pleased that you didn't go in after all because there are now 29,846,758 kids in there and incredible as it may seem, yet another four come along to join them. How can you find out how many are in the sandpit now?

- You could count all 29,846,762 of them.
- You could start counting at 29,846,758 and count up one number for each extra kid that comes in.

But just a minute! You've never practised counting past 29,846,758 before have you? (If you have then stop reading this book immediately and get urgent help.) In fact you've probably never even *seen* the number 29,846,758 before, so how do you know what it means? It's because you know about the number system which lets you understand any number immediately, which is one reason why maths is more fun than languages. If you suddenly came across words you had never seen before like "yeblidoob", "tzoon" and "glushjun" you wouldn't have the foggiest what they meant which is just as well as they are all a bit rude.

What's more, even if you have never seen the number 29,846,758 before, you can still count up from it, because you know that all you have to do is ADD ONE every time. Even though it's only adding one, it's still adding, and that counts as maths. Now be honest, did anybody ever tell you about counting by adding one at a time? No? In that case you must have worked out this little arithmetrick all by yourself! Who's a little clever pants then?

Before we move on to some serious sums, you'll be wondering how counting can be murderous – after all this is supposed to be a book about murderous maths. Right then, picture the scene. Your alarm clock has just gone off and with a happy smile you spring lightly out of bed. "Tra-lah," you sing to yourself as you get dressed, but just as you are reaching down for a sock, it twitches on the floor.

"Har har!" comes an evil voice from the top of the wardrobe. It's your arch enemy Professor Fiendish with a diabolically difficult mathematical trap.

HAR HAR!

13

"Har har!" he scowls again. "I've shoved thirteen deadly poisonous scorpions into your sock! What are you going to do about that then?"

Casually you tip the sock upside down and give it a deft flick. A selection of little bodies clatter on to the floor and scurry away. You count them up – and get twelve.

"Put it on then," sneers the professor.

"Not just yet I don't think!" you say with a wry smile.

With a final slick flick you eject the thirteenth scorpion up towards the crouching figure.

"Argh!" he wails as the scorpion embeds its long stinging tail in the professor's warty nose.

"Your plan was brilliant, Fiendish," you say as you nonchalantly pull on your sock. "And it would have worked – but for one tiny mistake. You didn't count on me being able to count."

So there you are. Even counting can be murderous. QED.

WHAT DOES QED MEAN?

You'll find out about QED and all sorts of other odd words and signs later. There's even such things as odd numbers which we'll find out about now.

Odd numbers

These are numbers that are *not even*. Gosh! What are even numbers then?

Even numbers

These are numbers that are *not odd*. There, that was helpful, wasn't it?

If you don't understand odd and even yet, then go and stand outside the cinema when there is a queue to see a really soppy love film. You can find out how many people are waiting to go in by just counting them up in the normal way: 1, 2, 3...

Once the film has started, go in and have a look round. Of course all the people will be frantically kissing each other, and in the dark all you will be able to make out are couples huddled together. It's a bit hard to count each person separately, but you can still find out how many people are there if you count the couples in TWOS! All you need to do is walk up and down the rows carrying a very full beaker of ice cold orange juice trying VERY HARD not to spill it on anybody. As you trip over the feet of each couple you count like this: 2, 4, 6...

Providing that absolutely everybody is involved with kissing another person, you will find there is what is called an EVEN number of people. Even numbers always end in 2,4,6,8 or 0. (So 44, 210 and 38,937,856 are all even numbers.)

BUT suppose you are just finishing counting all the couples and you suddenly see Pongo McWhiffy sitting by himself, you'll have to add an extra one to your number. This will give you an ODD number because you had to add an odd one, who was Pongo. Odd numbers always end in 1,3,5,7 or 9.

By the way, suppose the lovely Veronica Gumfloss came in and sat by Pongo, that would make another couple, so the number would then be even, and it would still be even even if Veronica sat by herself because if you add another odd one to an odd number, it becomes even. Odd, isn't it? Also if you add an odd one to any even number it becomes odd which is even odder.

Counting magic trick!

This extremely simple trick will catch out almost anybody. Ask your victim if he or she can count. The answer is bound to be yes, so then ask:

"Quick – what number comes next: nine thousand and ninety-six, nine thousand and ninety-seven, nine thousand and ninety-eight, nine thousand and ninety-nine…?"

Try it out on yourself first, in fact do it right now. What number do you think comes next?

If you said "ten thousand" – then write the numbers out in sequence and see what the right answer really is! (Remember – the first number is NOT nine thousand nine hundred and ninety-six!)

Does counting count as maths?

Yes it does – but be warned! This next bit is SO SIMPLE, you might not understand it.

If you wanted to explain to a pure mathematician what "three" means, the clearest thing to do is to count up – one, two, three! (Be warned though, the pure mathematician is quite likely to offer you a cup of strong coffee, sit you down and ask "Aha! But what do you mean by one and two?" and "Are you sure they always come in that order?" and even "What comes before one?" Honestly, although they can be lovely people, they're nutters, the lot of them.)

What is the difference between a number and a digit?

Before we get any older, we should clear this point up. There are ten different digits and they are: 1 2 3 4 5 6 7 8 9 0. You put digits together to make a number in the same way as you put letters together to make a word.

- The word "trousers" is only one word but it has eight letters.
- The number "4,789" is only one number but it has four digits.

Of course some words only have one letter such as when you are talking about yourself you say "I". Some numbers only have one digit – for instance how many nostrils have you got? The answer is 2. In this case 2 is the number of nostrils, but you only need a single digit to write it down. Not surprisingly, the digit is 2. It's clever stuff, isn't it?

One great thing about digits compared to letters – it's very hard to make spelling mistakes. Suppose you are counting, what number comes after 37? The answer is 38, which is very hard to spell wrong with digits. Of course if you use letters, you have lots of chances to make yourself look foolish:

THIRTEE ATE

THURTY AYT

FIRTY EIHGT

AWFUL ADDITION

Whether you're just adding one at a time, or working out mega sums that involve adding hundreds and thousands of numbers, there is one essential arithmetricks...

> **You can only add things that are the same.**

But there is also one handy trick to know...

> **It doesn't matter what order you add things in.**

For instance, suppose you were sitting in the bath with four elephants, and two more elephants jumped in, you would end up sharing the bath with six elephants. This would also work the other way round, you could start off with two elephants in the bath, and let four more jump in, and once again you'd end up sharing the bath with six elephants.

Written in numbers we're just saying that $4+2$ is the same as $2+4$ and they both come to 6. By the way, one of the great things about murderous maths is that if you don't believe what you read in this book, you can always try these experiments out for yourself. You'll find this one works perfectly – your only problem might be in finding out which elephant is sitting on the soap.

So much for adding up things that are the same, but now let's say that you have eight miniature poodles and put them in a cage with four crocodiles.

What have you got then?
- Twelve crocodiles?
- Twelve poodles?
- A mixture of crocodiles and poodles, which you could call twelve animals?
- Four very happy burping crocodiles who are ready for a quiet snooze?

You get the point.

Even if you are just adding up numbers for the sake of it, this trick of only adding things that are the same still applies. Let's add these numbers together: $324+61$.

The problem is that you have added things that are not the same. Ooh, naughty!

Something you didn't know you knew

There is an essential arithmetrick which says...

> **Each digit in a number means something different.**

If you can write down numbers bigger than nine, then you already knew this trick although you might not have realized it. To find out exactly what it means, have a look at the number two thousand and three which looks like this: 2,003. So which digit is worth more – the "2" or the "3"? Of course standing on their own "3" is worth more than "2", but in the number 2,003 the "2" actually means two thousand, and the "3" is just worth three units. (Or you can call it three "ones", or even just "three" if you like.) So how do we know the "2" is worth so much more? It's because of where it is placed.

To explain this, we're very lucky to have Wally the "1" to demonstrate.

Hang on, Wally! How do we know you've moved one place to the left? You're still on your own!

That's no good! We can't tell if that's an empty place, or if it's just a bit of blank paper. To stop it being confusing, Mr Postgate has kindly agreed to draw a zero in to show that it's an empty place.

THAT'S CLEVER! THAT ZERO MEANS THERE ARE NO UNITS AND IT ALSO SHOWS THAT I'M STANDING IN THE 'TENS' PLACE. LIKE I SAID, HERE I'M WORTH TEN.

I'VE MOVED OVER ANOTHER PLACE, HERE I'M WORTH A HUNDRED!

And we've put in another zero for you, Wally.

AND EVERY PLACE I MOVE TO THE LEFT, I'M WORTH TEN TIMES MORE!

AAAAGHH!

Thank you, Wally, that was lovely.

Now then, let's get a groovy number like 5,894,732 and here you can see what each digit is really worth:

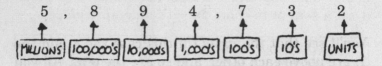

(Incidentally, people put the little commas in just to make it easier to see what a big number is with a quick glance. They show you where the thousands and even the millions start. You can leave them out if you like and get 5894732 which is more useful when you are getting on with the sums.)

What we're saying is that you can't just add up all the digits in a number like you did, because they all mean something different. In fact if you attacked this big number and added up $5 + 8 + 9 + 4 + 7 + 3 + 2$ then you end up with a thing called a "digital root" which is a complete waste of time when you're trying to work out something interesting and sensible like how many hairs you've got or how many chips you've eaten in your whole life.

Let's go back to the sum and see what's REALLY going on. It looked like this: $324 + 61$, but to help us keep the different bits apart, we usually write sums down like this:

24

$$324$$
$$+ \ \underline{\ 61}$$
$$= \ \underline{\ \ \ }$$

You'll see that the units (in this case the 4 and the 1) are above each other, and so are the tens. All you do is add up the units and you get $4 + 1 = 5$, so you write 5 underneath in the answer box. Then you add up the tens so you get $2 + 6 = 8$, and you put the 8 in the answer box. The three hundreds don't have anything to add to, so they just go straight into the answer box, and you get...

$$324$$
$$+ \ \underline{\ 61}$$
$$= \underline{385}$$

There's another way of looking at this. You can split each number into its separate bits then add them up, so $324 + 61$ becomes $300 + 20 + 4 + 60 + 1$. Because it's all addition, you can move the numbers round and get $300 + 20 + 60 + 4 + 1$, then all you do is add the units, the tens and the hundreds separately. You get $300 + 80 + 5$, and when you put it back together you get 385. Dead easy.

SO YOU THINK YOU'RE SO CLEVER, EH? TRY THIS ONE!..

Gosh, he wants us to add three numbers all together! Actually, there's no problem here because addition is about the only thing in maths where you can deal with more than two numbers at once. What's more to the point is that most addition sums give us an extra thrill that we haven't come across yet, so here's how to deal with it...

First we'll write the numbers out in a nice convenient pile like this:

$$
\begin{array}{r}
417 \\
+\ 48 \\
+189 \\
\hline
=\ \underline{}
\end{array}
$$

← A THRILLING GAP.

Because of this little extra thrill we're going to get, we'll need a bit of extra space somewhere, and most people leave a gap under the answer line.

Off we go then, we'll add up the units: $7 + 8 + 9$ comes to 24. Gosh, how thrilling! In our answer 24, we have 4 units – and also 2 tens! We write down the 4 units in the answer box, but what do we do with the 2 tens? It's no good just hoping that they'll go away, so what happens is that we "carry them over" into the tens column.

26

$$
\begin{array}{r}
417 \\
+\ 48 \\
+\ 189 \\
=\quad 4 \\
\hline
2
\end{array}
$$

← FILLING THE THRILLING GAP WITH 'CARRIED OVER' NUMBERS.

You'll see we've written the 2 tens as a little "2" in the thrilling gap underneath the tens column. We can now add up all the tens, *including the 2 tens we just carried over*! We get $1 + 4 + 8 + 2$ which comes to 15. Just as we did with the units we write down the 5 tens in the answer box, but we carry over the 10 tens (which make one hundred) by putting a little "1" in the hundreds place in the thrilling gap.

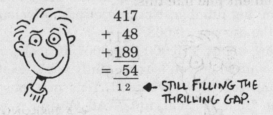

$$
\begin{array}{r}
417 \\
+\ 48 \\
+\ 189 \\
=\quad 54 \\
\hline
1\ 2
\end{array}
$$

← STILL FILLING THE THRILLING GAP.

We now add up the hundreds (including the one we carried over) and get $4 + 1 + 1$ which makes 6.

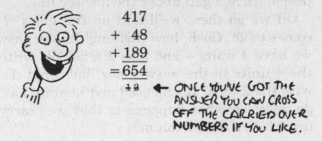

$$
\begin{array}{r}
417 \\
+\ 48 \\
+\ 189 \\
=654 \\
\hline
1\ 2
\end{array}
$$

← ONCE YOU'VE GOT THE ANSWER YOU CAN CROSS OFF THE CARRIED OVER NUMBERS IF YOU LIKE.

There – we've finished! Relax, take a shower, have a cup of tea and try to wind down a bit. This sort of excitement is great fun in short bursts, but you do have to be careful not to overdo it otherwise you'll be a cause for concern to your family and friends.

And suddenly we're clever!

As long as you remember about only adding things that are the same, some very long looking sums become simple to do, even in your head! How about this: 10,003 + 5. All you do is add the 5 to the units of the big number. Nothing else is affected, so you get the answer 10,008.

How about 170,000 + 30,000? It looks nasty at first, but when you look carefully you'll see that it is adding together seventeen "tens of thousands" to three "tens of thousands". All you do is work out 17 + 3 and get an answer of 20, which of course means twenty "tens of thousands". When you write it out you get 200,000 which you might realize is the same as two hundred thousand.

You might wonder why a posh book like this is bothering to make such a fuss about a bit of adding up, but understanding how the simple stuff works is vital whether you're doing maths or anything else. Suppose you fancy playing the Rachmaninov piano concerto in C minor at the Albert Hall – you've got no chance unless you first learnt how to open the piano lid.

Of course for our nutty chums the pure mathematicians, there's no such thing as simple stuff. It took thousands of years for them all to agree that if you add nothing to any number, the answer is that same number. In other words when they finally worked out that $5 + 0 = 5$, they were all terribly proud of themselves, bless 'em.

As you've gathered by now, even with the simplest addition you should...

Write numbers above each other so that all the units are in the same column.

Of course if you get the units lined up, then this ensures that your tens are lined up, so are the hundreds and the thousands and so on. You can easily see why this is a good thing because which of these looks easier to add up?

29

One special case is if you are adding up money – say you're going round the shops wondering what you can afford for Christmas presents. Again, it's worth trying to keep different amounts directly above each other.

£3.50
28p
£11.35
80p

Here you can see single pennies are in a column, "tens" of pennies are in a column, so are single pounds and "tens" of pounds.

Other ways of saying addition
Because adding things up is so common, there are lots of different ways of saying it.

- You can add up a set of numbers.
- You can get the total of a set of numbers.
- You can find the sum of a set of numbers.

And finally ... a joke about addition that your teacher never told you:

RALPH'S FIRST ARITHMETIC LESSON!

SOME SNEAKY SIGNS

...and how to get all your homework sums right every time!

Maths is full of signs which tell you what to do and how everything works, so let's look at the ones we've used so far.

BUT WE'VE ONLY HAD 'PLUS' AND 'EQUALS'

Oh really? So you haven't noticed the INVISIBLE signs then?

EH?

One of the main arithmetricks is knowing how to use, move and swap signs about, so we'll start with the easiest ones and see what they really do.

= EQUALS

Just about every sum in the world has to have an equals sign, and when you write sums out in a line like this: $28 + 4 + 9 = 41$ they get called EQUATIONS. Luckily for us, the equals sign is nice and straightforward, it just tells us that all the stuff on one side of the equation equals all the stuff on the other side.

To explain it properly let's go to the park and find a see-saw.

Let's pretend that our equals sign is the pivot in the middle of the see-saw, and that everything on one side has to balance with everything on the other side. The pivot doesn't actually add any weight to either side, but of course if you took it away then everything would collapse in a heap. So the equals sign is very important but it doesn't actually DO anything. (Some headteachers are like equals signs because they stride around being "very important" but they don't actually do anything either. You know the sort, but the less about them, the better.)

Right, let's find some things to put on the see-saw. First of all we'll have the same number on both sides:

We've got five penguins on each side, so they balance. This is just like having an equation which says $5 = 5$.

Why don't you mark this page by folding the corner over or something? Then if EVER you think maths has just got too mind-numbingly miserable and you are weeping in despair, you could come back to this page, look at this nice little equation, suck your thumb and realize life isn't so bad after all.

Oh no! Two of our penguins have waddled off the see-saw. That leaves one side with just three left.

You'll notice our see-saw isn't balanced any more, obviously because 5 does not equal 3. However, this gives us a chance to use another sign:

≠ NOT EQUALS

Rather conveniently, this sign looks like a picture of a see-saw that is lower at one side than the other. (Well, it does if you turn it sideways and use your imagination.) This sign is also a brilliant way of getting all your maths homework right:

$$13 + 7 \neq 2$$
$$5 + 12 \neq 2$$
$$23 + 6 \neq 26$$
$$4 + 8 \neq 1$$
$$6 + 2 \neq 16$$

The teacher might not like it, but in fact there's no mistakes there!

Here's another sign that could come in handy if you're not sure about an equation:

≈ ROUGHLY EQUALS
If you're adding together a few big numbers and can't be bothered to do it exactly you could put this: $246 + 65 + 687 \approx 1000$

It's a bit cheeky, but technically there's nothing actually wrong with it. This sign is especially handy for when you are doing "rough sums" which we'll find out about later on.

Getting back to the proper equals sign, why doesn't our equation work any more? The answer lies in one of the most crucial arithmetricks:

> **You must treat both sides of an equation exactly the same.**

What went wrong was that two penguins got off one side but no penguins got off the other side – so one side of the see-saw got treated differently from the other. If we want to balance up the wonky see-saw, we have two choices: adding or subtracting.

Adding
Oh. We've got a little problem: the penguins have been scared away by the monkeys. Never mind, the numbers are the same so on we go. We have five on one side, and three on the other, but we'll ADD two more to the three.

35

Everything has balanced up again, and it has given us the equation $5 = 3 + 2$, and rather excitingly we've used the "$+$" sign.

+ PLUS

The plus sign is telling us to do a job with the number that comes after it. In this case we have "$+ 2$" which tells us to add two more monkeys. You'll see that a plus sign is different to "equals" because it actually does something, and signs that do things are called "operators". The trick is that...

Any operator sign must stay with the number that comes after it.

Otherwise you won't know what to do. If you had a sum that said $56 + =$ you'd be stuck wouldn't you?

Subtracting

Gosh, the monkeys have been scared off by the lions now, and as before we have five on one side and three on the other so it doesn't balance.

This time we can't balance the see-saw by adding two more lions on, so instead we'll take two away.

This gives us the equation $5 - 2 = 3$ and here we meet...

– MINUS

This little sign is the "take away" or "minus" sign. It does the opposite job to "plus" because with "plus" you have to put things together, but with "minus" you have to split them up. The minus sign is also an operator, and so it must always stay with the number that comes after it. In the equation we just saw it tells us to "take away 2" lions.

Negative numbers

Here's two things to know...

> **Numbers with a *plus* in front are called *positive* numbers.**
>
> **Numbers with a *minus* in front are called *negative* numbers.**

Negative numbers are used to describe all sorts of things from borrowing money to running backwards, but all we need to know here is that negative numbers make positive numbers smaller when you put them together. Here's a simple example:

Suppose you were an ant walking along the ground with some other ants, you could describe your height above the ground as zero.

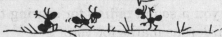

However, if you climbed up on to a dustbin, your height might then be one metre above ground. This is brilliant because you could grab on to the dustbin handle with your tiny little anty legs and bounce along DOINK BLUNK KADDUNK, waving down at the other ants and scaring them to bits as you shout:

The trouble is that you won't be looking where you are going and suddenly the dustbin (with you on it) is bound to fall down a hole one metre deep. Because the hole goes down rather than up, you could describe the height of the hole as "−1 metre". This negative value of one metre subtracts itself from your positive height of one metre and so your height gets reduced back down to zero.

This is bad news because now that your height is zero again, all the other ants will come charging over and give you a sound biffing for scaring them. Still, that's murderous maths for you.

How to make equations prettier

In the same way that your Great Auntie Doris might like moving her ornaments around the mantelpiece to make them look prettier, you can move the numbers round equations to make them look prettier too.

Look at the equation we had with the monkeys. It was $5 = 3 + 2$.

Obviously the 2 has a + sign, but what about the other numbers? Well this is the spooky bit, because they have *invisible plus signs*.

In the same way that every operator needs a number to stick to, every number also needs an operator. If you can't see a sign in front of a number, you can assume it has an invisible $+$. If we wanted to make the invisible signs visible we could do this ... $+5 = +3 + 2$ ... but we don't usually bother writing out plus signs that come at the front.

Now that we know about these operators, it's easy to see how we can move the numbers round. The first trick is...

> **You can move numbers where you like so long as you don't move them across the equals sign to the other side.**

This means that we can swap round the $+3$ and the $+2$ to get $+5 = +2 + 3$. Of course, you can make the plus signs at the front invisible again if you like to get $5 = 2 + 3$.

Now let's look at the lions equation: $5 - 2 = 3$

Can you swap the 5 and 2 round to get $2 - 5 = 3$? No, of course not, because we've forgotten that an operator must stay with the number after it, so the take-away sign must stay with the 2. If you swap round the 5 and 2 properly you get: $-2 + 5 = 3$.

You'll notice that the invisible + in front of the 5 isn't invisible any more! Also, you must not make the − invisible otherwise you wouldn't know if it was an invisible + or an invisible − or even an invisible Gollark from the planet Zog for that matter.

Now then, let's look at the monkey equation AND the lion equation:

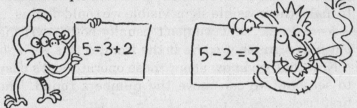

Can you see the difference between them?

Yes − the number 2 has swapped sides − and its sign has changed from plus to minus! This happened because we treated both sides of the equation the same way.

It happens like this. You start with $5 = 3 + 2$. Then you take away 2 from both sides and get: $5 − 2 = 3 + 2 − 2$.

Now, get ready for some *good news*…

Yes indeed, you'll notice that sitting together at the end of our equation are $+2$ and $−2$. This is the sort of thing that gets mathematicians really excited, because two take away two obviously leaves nothing so we can just cross them off and forget them. This is called cancelling out and it leaves us with this: $5 − 2 = 3$.

What we've just done is the long version of another nifty little arithmetrick which works for simple equations...

> **You CAN move a number across to the other side BUT ONLY if you change its sign.**
> (This means you change a + to a − or you change a − to a +.)

There's one more trick to know, and for this we'll go back to the see-saw.

Er ... well this rather strange equation seems to work because the see-saw has balanced. Whoops! There go the vultures...

That's interesting: the see-saw is still balanced because both sides lost a vulture. As we said before, as long as you treat both sides the same, you won't have any problems.

Now then, everybody else on the see-saw has to swap sides.

At last they have all crossed over.

As you can see, the see-saw is balanced again which demonstrates another trick:

If you want to you can swap both sides of an equation over.

Oh no, now the elephant wants to join in, but where can she go? Remember, we have to treat both sides the same...

The right order

In a minute we're going to get an ugly equation and beautify it with a mathematical make-over, but before we do here's something that you might be wondering. Suppose you have to work out a sum like this: $11 - 4 + 5 = ?$

You might think that there are two ways you could do it. Do you...

- take away the 4 from the 11 (to get 7) then add on the 5 to get an answer of 12?

Or do you...

- add the 5 to the 4 (to get 9) then take it away from the 11 to get an answer of 2?

Obviously they can't both be right, so which is it?

In fact the first option is correct, as we'll find out from a little story called "The History Essay".

When you have sums to work out like this...

$$12 - 7 - 1 + 5 - 3 + 1 = ?$$

...you can't go far wrong if you just work along from left to right. In this case you get a set of simple sums as follows: $12 - 7 = 5$ then $5 - 1 = 4$ then $4 + 5 = 9$ then $9 - 3 = 6$ and finally $6 + 1 = 7$.

Sometimes you hit a nasty little problem like this...

$$4 - 7 - 1 + 9 = ?$$

To work it out you would start with $4 - 7 = -3$ as your first sum. Your next sum is then $-3 - 1 = ?$ Urgh! Does it come to -4 or -2? Think about it like this. You are an ant again and the other ants have just thrown you down a hole three metres deep (so your "height" is -3 metres). You walk around the bottom of the hole and suddenly fall into another hole which is one metre deep. How deep are you altogether? Yes, you're now 4 metres deep, so your "height" is -4 metres.

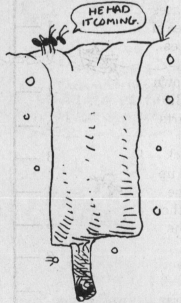

HE HAD IT COMING.

In other words if you put -3 and -1 together, you get -4.

Luckily this negative mess can sometimes be avoided by moving the positive numbers to the front of your sum before you start. In this case you'd get...

$$4 + 9 - 7 - 1 = ?$$

But that's enough sums for now. Grab a friend or two and let's all have a game...

Frazzle or fish food?

Once you've got the basics of adding and subtracting little numbers sorted out, here's a challenge for you.

What you need:
- 21 playing cards – the ace, 2, 3, 4, 5 of each suit and a joker.
- A counter for each player.

How to play:
- Shuffle the cards and put them face down.
- Players start with their counters beside the boat.
- Players take turns to take a card from the pack. If you get:
  a black card – you move upwards the number of places on the card (so for the three of clubs, move up three places).

  a red card – you move down the number of places on the card (so for the ace of hearts move down one place).

  the joker – you move back to the boat. You also pick up all the cards (including the joker) and shuffle them, then put them face down for the game to continue.
- If you hit the sun you are frazzled to bits!
- If you reach the shark, you get eaten!
- The last person left alive is the winner.

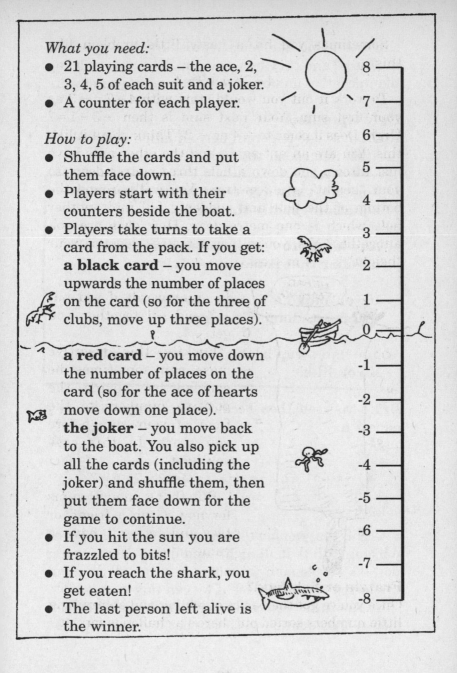

47

(In this game the black cards are like "positive numbers" and they move you up. The red cards are like "negative numbers" and they move you down.)

Ugly equations

Right, it's time to get an ugly equation and make it prettier. Remember the tricks...

> **You must always treat both sides of an equation exactly the same.**
>
> **Any operator sign must stay with the number that comes after it.**
>
> **If you move a number to the other side, you must change its sign.**
>
> **You can swap both sides over completely if you like.**

Brace yourself then because here comes the ugly equation:

$$5 + 7 - 10 + 12 + 1 = 11 - 6 + 5 - 1 + 6$$

Urgh! You wouldn't fancy going to a party and dancing with that all night, would you? No, of course not. It's got too many numbers in it and all the signs are mixed up, so let's see if we can tidy it up a bit.

If you wanted you could work out the value of each side of the equation to check that it is correct. (You

48

should find that both sides equal 15.) However, it's more fun to *simplify* it first, which means making it prettier and easier to work out. First we'll move the numbers round on each side, remembering to keep them attached to their operators.

$$12 + 1 + 5 + 7 - 10 = 11 + 5 + 6 - 6 - 1$$

Hang on, here's *more good news...*

Yes indeed! Prepare to cheer because we've managed to get $+6$ and -6 together on the same side, so we can get rid of them.

$$12 + 1 + 5 + 7 - 10 = 11 + 5 - 1$$

HOORAY! It's looking simpler already.

The next thing we notice is that both sides have a $+5$. Well, we are allowed to treat both sides the same, so if we take the $+5$ away from one side, we can take the $+5$ away from the other.

$$12 + 1 + 7 - 10 = 11 - 1$$

HOORAY AGAIN!

Now you'll see that one side has $+1$ and the other has -1, so can these cancel out? Sadly no, you can only cancel them out if they are on the same side. Never mind, let's move one of them across (don't forget to change the sign) and get this:

$$12 + 1 + 1 + 7 - 10 = 11$$

What else would you like to do? If you're in a "I hate minus signs" mood you can just move the 10 across to get:

$$12 + 1 + 1 + 7 = 11 + 10$$

A different thing that some people like to do is to make one side into zero. All you need to do here is move the 11 across which leaves you with nothing on the right-hand side. Don't leave it blank though or it looks like this:

$$12 + 1 + 1 + 7 - 10 - 11 =$$

Anybody who sees that might think that you had got yourself so excited writing out your equation that you wet your pants and had to rush off to the bathroom before you had time to finish it. That's why you'll find that all the greatest mathematicians such as Pythagoras, Euclid, de Fermat, Euler and co. were never called "wet knickers" because they always made sure they put a "0" in like this:

$$12 + 1 + 1 + 7 - 10 - 11 = 0$$

Whatever you want to do to your equations, as long as you stick to the rules, they will always work. You can check any of these prettier equations that we've made, and you'll find they are fine.

Murderous medicine

Gosh! It's lucky you know about these tricks because you have just been bitten by a fearsome two-headed Arctic ice snake.

Already your blood is starting to freeze solid, but in front of you is a cabinet of mathematically prepared antidotes which were all made up from the equation:

$$3909 + 178 - 1419 = 6077 - 3425 + 16$$

Three of these bottles have correct equations on them, but the fourth could be LETHAL! You haven't time to work all the sums out, but by altering the original formula using the tricks, can you see which three equations are correct? That way you can find the bottle with the wrong formula, and so avoid drinking the murderous medicine!

Right, that'll have to be enough about signs and equations for now because something new and slightly nasty has rather cleverly sneaked in. Did you spot it? Here it is again:

It looks innocent enough but if you magnify it a few million times it looks like this:

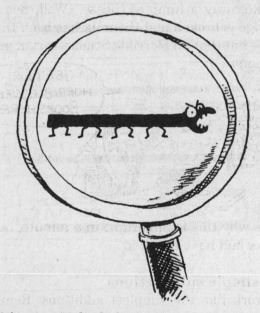

True, it's a nasty little beast, but don't worry. A few cunning arithmetricks will soon sort it out, so read on...

Sickly Subtraction

The same essential arithmetrick applies to subtraction as addition:

> **You can only take away things that are the same.**

If you've only got six pints of milk in the fridge, you can't take away a lump of cheese. (Well, not unless your fridge is broken and the milk has been there for months – but that's a Horrible Science sort of problem so we'll ignore it.)

We'll see why this is important in a minute, but first let's relax and have a look at...

Really simple subtractions

These work like the simplest additions. Remember what happened when there were 35 people in the sandpit and four more got in? You just had to count up one number for each new person like this: 36, 37, 38, 39. You can do the same with simple subtractions.

Suppose you have 51 people in the sandpit and suddenly 5 of them dig down and find something white and shiny with little bits of wispy hair on it.

They immediately shout "Hey! We've found a skull!" and all five of them run off to find a candle to put in it to make a tasteful table decoration for dinner parties.

The problem is, how many kids are left in the sandpit hoping to find other buried body parts? The sum looks like this: $51 - 5 = ?$ To work it out, you just count down one number for each person that leaves. You start with 51, then count down one for the first leaver, so that comes to 50. Keep counting down as the other people leave and you get 49, 48, 47 and finally you get to the answer, which is 46.

Of course just as the excitement has settled down, several giant bony hands with long yellow finger-nails thrust up out of the sand and grab on to some of the kids.

Forty-two of them manage to get away, but how many kids are caught and pulled under the sand and down into the undiscovered Zombie ghetto that always exists underneath sandpits?

We had 46 kids to start with, but 42 got away so the sum looks like this $46 - 42 = ?$ To work it out you could start at 46 and count down 42 places, but now we know about moving equations about, we can think of a quicker way. Instead of $46 - 42 = ?$ we just move the 42 over to make an addition sum: $46 = 42 + ?$

This is like asking, how many numbers do we have to count on to 42 to make 46? Simple, we just count up and we get 43, 44, 45 and then 46. We have counted up four numbers, so that's how many kids are being transmuted into undead ghouls forever destined to live under sandpits luring other un-suspecting prey to their doom.

I HATE DAYS LIKE THESE.

Of course, counting is only useful for sums where one of the numbers is quite small. What if you had a sum like this: $81 - 48 = ?$

This is too much to count, especially if you were using your fingers. You would have to take your socks off and use your toes too AND you'd have to borrow somebody else's fingers and toes as well.

28, 29, 30

This can get a bit embarrassing in places like the supermarket, so let's see if we can work it out with a bit of common sense.

To start with, it's handy to rearrange the sum to look like this: $81 = 48 + ?$ You don't actually need to write this down, all you are doing is asking yourself "what number would I need to add to 48 to make 81?" You can work this out in easy bits.

First you could say that:

$48 + 2 = 50.$ ← Here you've added 2.

Then say:

$50 + 30 = 80.$ ← Now you've added 30 more.

Finally you do:

$80 + 1 = 81.$ ← You've added another 1.

So how much did you need to add on altogether?

It was $2 + 30 + 1$ which altogether makes 33. That's the answer! $81 - 48 = 33$. With a bit of practice, you should be able to do sums like this in your head.

When you get into even bigger subtractions, you'll find they also work like bigger additions. How about this: $459 - 312 = ?$

As we've found out, the trick is that you can only take away things that are the same, so first we'll just deal with the units and get $9 - 2 = 7$. Then you deal with the tens and get $5 - 1 = 4$ and finally the hundreds, $4 - 3 = 1$. Put them together (in the right order!) and get an answer of 147. That was too easy, so let's crack another ... $371 - 4 = ?$

It's a simple enough sum, but to do it properly, first we do the units and get $1 - 4 = -3$ ... oh dear! In fact what we need to do is "borrow" an extra ten from the 371 so that the 1 becomes 11, then you can take the 4 away, but where does the borrowed ten come from?

56

Well funnily enough, you'll find out as we rush off to...

City: Chicago, Illinois, U.S.A.
Place: Luigi's Diner, Upper Main Street
Date: 28 August, 1926
Time: 9:45 p.m.

Luigi sweated as he checked his table list again. How could it have happened? Both of the rival mob families had been booked into his diner on the same night. For two hours the Gabriannis had been sitting at their favourite table by the lavatory door (handy for a rear window escape if the police came in the front). Any minute now the Boccellis could arrive and the inevitable fight could put the whole place out of business for months.

Luigi nudged Benni the waiter and tapped his watch meaningfully. Benni understood and nervously approached the four figures hunched around the dirty pudding plates.

"Can I fetch your coats, gentlemen?" he asked.

"You hurrying us?" snapped Half-smile Gabrianni.

"N-no!" stammered Benni. "It's just I'm waiting to clear up."

"And you can keep waiting," sneered Chainsaw Charlie. "After all, you're a waiter ain't ya?"

There was a guffaw of laughter.

"While you're waiting you can get us some more of these breadsticks," said Numbers, indicating the empty basket on the table.

From behind the counter Luigi saw Benni hurry towards him. Luigi groaned. He had had five complete cases of breadsticks before the Gabriannis had sat down, but they had eaten so many he found himself keeping a careful record of what he had left.

"Jeez!" moaned Luigi. "Is that all gangsters do these days? Eat breadsticks?"

"This stick on the counter, is it the only one we got left?" asked Benni.

"Not quite," said Luigi as he reached for his notepad and checked the figures:

Cases	Packets	Sticks
3	7	1

"At least they pack them sensibly," said Luigi. "There's ten sticks in a packet and ten packets in a case. It's easy to see there's 371 breadsticks left in total."

"Right," said Benni. "Only there isn't because we're about to give them a whole lot more."

"Just ONE more," snapped Luigi. "Well, one more each but that's enough. We don't want them hanging around eating breadsticks if the Boccellis are due in any minute."

"So one stick each makes four sticks I gotta take over," said Benni, "but how can I do that when there's only one loose one?"

"You'll just have to open up another new packet," said Luigi. "So instead of having seven packets left unopened, I'll just have six."

Benni opened the packet and tipped the ten fresh breadsticks on to the counter next to the single one.

"Ten plus one makes eleven," said Benni. "But not for long because I'm taking four away."

As Benni set off, Luigi counted up the sticks on the counter.

"Seven left," he sighed, and scribbled some new notes on his pad.

Cases	Packets	Sticks
3	7	1

(Benni takes away four)

3	6	7

"Well there's a thing!" muttered Luigi to himself. "371 take away four makes 367. Hey! I could even work out how many they've eaten altogether! I started with five complete cases, so if I just take away 367..."

But Luigi was interrupted by the crash of the door bursting open. Two men stepped inside.

"Oh no, they're here!" gasped Luigi as he ducked down behind the counter.

"Glad to see you too, Luigi!" sneered Blade Boccelli. "Hey Benni, you wanna get this place cleaned up. There's vermin crawling all over our favourite table."

"I'll clean you up, you punk," snarled Chainsaw leaping to his feet.

"That's my brother you're talking to," said One Finger Jimmy. "If you so much as lay a finger on him…"

"…then you'll lay a finger on me?" sniggered Chainsaw. "Let's face it. That's all you can do. You only got the one."

"You watch it," said Blade. "Anything you Gabriannis do, we can do bigger."

"Oh yeah?" chorused the men round the table.

"Yeah. We hound you more, we hit you more, we hurt you more…"

"But I bet you can't eat more breadsticks," muttered Benni.

"What?" said Blade.

"Er ... it's these breadsticks," stuttered Benni. "These guys sure can eat a lot."

"Yeah, because we're lots-of-breadstick-eating kind of guys," boasted the weasel.

"What say we just shoot 'em up?" said Jimmy.

"No, wait," said Blade. "That gets kind of boring."

"Yeah, and it hurts too," muttered Half-smile.

Everybody nodded. At least they all agreed on one thing, that being shot could be quite painful.

"So what's with this breadsticks thing?" asked Jimmy.

"Forget it," said Weasel. "We've been sitting here eating breadsticks all night. You'll never eat more than we did."

Blade smiled. "Oh no? Maybe you forgot our secret weapon."

A large shadow passed the window, and then the edge of a stomach appeared in the doorway.

"Our little brother was just parking the car," explained Blade. "In you come, Porky."

The third Boccelli brother came in. Not all at once, but stepping sideways and slowly easing himself through the frame.

"Did somebody mention breadsticks?" he grinned.

"Hey, but that's not fair!" moaned Half-smile.

"He's like six people sharing one pair of pants!" muttered Numbers.

"Us three against you four – is that a problem for you?" sneered Blade.

The four Gabriannis all gulped together which actually sounded quite funny but nobody was laughing.

"Because", continued Blade, "just to make it interesting, if we win, you pay for our dinner tonight. What do you say?"

"No problem," stammered the Weasel. "And if you lose, you pay for ours."

Blade snapped his fingers.

"Breadsticks, Benni," he said. "Keep 'em coming and keep 'em counted. We'll soon see who does things biggest round here."

Luigi sighed as Benni hurried towards him. At least giving away breadsticks was cheaper than fixing the windows and furniture.

It was some hours later when a massive booming sound rattled the shutters.

Blade woke up, and raised his head. Around him most of the others were slumped over and snoring, indeed only Porky and Luigi seemed to have kept awake.

"Hey, Porky," Blade yawned, "you finished at last?"

Porky blinked and smiled. A few solitary crumbs fluttered down from his chin.

"So what's the score, Luigi?" asked Blade.

Luigi checked his pad.

"Well, before I started tonight I had five hundred sticks, but after the others had finished I only had 367 left. I make it that they ate 133."

"Holy trousers!" gasped Jimmy as he sat up and had a good stretch and a bit of a scratch. "I didn't realize we had so many to beat! How did we do?"

"Well," said Luigi, "I got two cases, three packets and five singles left, which is 235. I got to take that from the 367 to get your score."

"OK, OK!" moaned Blade. "Enough maths already. Who pays the bill, us or them?"

Luigi did the sum, then checked it.

"Look, Blade," he said apologetically, "they're all asleep, maybe you guys just want to eat a couple more?"

"Why?" asked Blade, but then the truth dawned on him. "You mean they beat us at eating breadsticks?"

Luigi nodded nervously.

"The shame of it!" sobbed Porky.

"They're asleep," said Luigi. "You guys only managed to eat 132, but I could tell a lie if you want."

"No," said Blade shaking his head slowly. "You're a good guy, Luigi, you're a man of honour. I couldn't ask you to lie. Sure, I might ask you to poison somebody then keep the stiff in your freezer until the heat's off, but asking you to lie is going too far. Here's the money. Me and my brothers we'll just quietly get up and go. I don't want to face those guys laughing at us."

Luigi watched amazed as the three Boccellis quietly let themselves out and disappeared down the street.

OH! THE HUMILIATION!

"Look, Benni!" he said shaking the waiter's shoulder and waving the money under his face. "Blade paid up!"

Benni roused himself and as he did, four breadsticks fell from his pocket.

"What is it?" he asked rubbing his eyes, but Luigi was staring at the floor.

"Never mind what it is!" gasped Luigi. "What are those?"

"Those?" asked Benni. "Oh those! Those are the four breadsticks I was taking over to the Gabriannis. I guess they never got them."

"They never got them!" gasped Luigi. "Wow!"

"Never got what?" drawled Half-smile as he sat up.

"You never got these extra breadsticks you ordered," said Luigi.

"Breadsticks?" asked the Weasel rubbing his eyes. "That reminds me, who won?"

"Well," said Luigi, "they ate 132, and you ordered 133..."

"Great!" said Chainsaw.

"...but you never actually ate these four, so they don't count!"

"133 less four is 129," said Numbers. "So we just ate 129."

"You mean ... they beat us?" gasped Half-smile.

"Shhh!" said the Weasel. "The less said about this the better. Luigi, here's enough money to cover the bills and keep your mouth shut. Come on you guys, let's scram."

The door closed behind them.

"What was all that about?" asked Benni.

"That was all about subtraction!" grinned Luigi waving two handfuls of money. "And you know what? I LOVE it!"

A good job for subtraction

Subtraction is very handy for helping you check your change in shops. For instance if you buy a pot of maggots for £3.79 and pay with a £5 note, what change should you get?

£5.00	money you paid
− £3.79	what it cost
= £1.21	the change you should get

Remember to write the numbers directly above each other just like in addition.

You can always check subtractions too, you just add the bottom two numbers and see if you get the top one. In this case you can work out £1.21 + £3.79 and hopefully you'll find it comes to £5.

If it doesn't then write to the *Murderous Maths* factory and complain that it's wrong, then the factory workers will have to go round every house in the whole world asking for any copies of this book and collecting up every single one and then they'll have to take them all back for re-printing, and then set off and hand out posh new copies to everybody and it will cost millions. Still, that's what customers expect these days.

AT LEAST WE'll SAVE ON OUR HEATING BILLS.

The take-away menu

Look at this sum: $15 - 9 = ?$ If you like you can call it 15 take away 9, but you've a lot more choice than that...

- You can subtract 9 from 15.
- You can reduce 15 by 9.
- You can find the difference between 15 and 9.
- You could have 15 and knock off 9.
- And of course it's also 15 minus 9.

A CRACKING CODE!

Addition and subtraction have lots of uses, and one of the best is for sending coded messages. Before you start you have to write out your message, then swap each letter for a number. The simplest way to swap them is this:

A	B	C	D	E	F	G
1	2	3	4	5	6	7

H	I	J	K	L	M	N
8	9	10	11	12	13	14

O	P	Q	R	S	T	U
15	16	17	18	19	20	21

V	W	X	Y	Z
22	23	24	25	26

Suppose you wanted to say "Hello Granny", it would come out like this:

8 5 12 12 15 7 18 1 14 14 25

(When writing codes you tend to ignore any spaces.)

To ENCODE your message you use addition and you also need to have a KEY number. This can be any number you like, but you should only tell it to the person who is receiving the message.

Let's say the key number for this message is 11.

What you do is write the key number in front of the message...

```
ll  8  5  12  12  15  7  18  1  14  14  25
```

...then add up each number with the one that comes after it. So for your coded message you have $11 + 8 = 19$ then $8 + 5 = 13$, then $5 + 12 = 17$ and so on. Here's the coded message all ready to send:

```
19  13  17  24  27  22  25  19  15  28  39
```

This is a very tough code to break if you don't know the key number! (It would be even tougher if you had scrambled up what numbers you use for each letter, say $A = 13$ and $B = 7$ and so on. But remember that if you scramble up the letters and numbers, the person who gets the message must know how you've done it.)

To DECODE the message, you need to write the key number under the first number of the coded message, then subtract it. (In this case you get $19 - 11 = 8$) You then take the answer away from the second number (here you get $13 - 8 = 5$), and keep going to the end.

```
  19  13  17  24  27  22  25  19  15  28  39
- 11   8   5  12
=  8   5  12           and so on...
```

68

The original coded message will appear along the bottom!

Remember to tell the KEY NUMBER only to the person you are sending the message to. You could even have a system where the key number keeps changing. How about using the day of the month as the key number – that way your number changes every day!

A bit later in this book there is a joke that is SO RUDE that it had to be coded, otherwise all the people working in *Murderous Maths* bookshops would have been arrested and given five years of geography homework.

For extra security you have to work out the key number to decode it yourself – which gives you some idea of how rude this joke is.

Right, it's time for some *even more good news*!

All we've done so far in this book is look at addition and subtraction. You might have thought it was all too easy to bother with, but here's an astounding fact:

**ALMOST ANY CALCULATION
CAN BE DONE PURELY BY USING
ADDITION AND SUBTRACTION.**

Amazing but true! Of course you are now wondering why we should be bothered with anything else. The answer is that everything else in this book is a SHORT CUT. For instance, you could work this horrid sum out purely with addition and subtraction:

$$235,894 \times 4,388 \div 974 = ?$$

But it would probably take you months, you would be covering bits of paper the size of Jamaica and it would drive you utterly mental. That's why it's worth making the bit of effort required to overcome...

THE TERRIBLE TABLES

You can tell how miserable learning the times tables is by the wonderful variety of different ways teachers try and make it interesting. Here's how they did it in the old days:

And here's some of the ways they do it these days:

Cutesy

Musical

Sad

Cop out

Who knows what they will try next, eh? Still, you'd better enjoy it while you can because all this playing about is just a phase teachers are going through. It can't be long before a highly advanced alien civilization will cross the universe to contact us, and amongst the other great benefits they will bestow upon mankind will be their far superior teaching methods which look like this...

Down to the nitty-gritty

The tables are all you need to know to do simple multiplications and divisions in your head. As we said before, you could do these sorts of sums just using addition and subtraction if you like, but it's a bit sad. Look...

Six ladies eat nine cakes each. How many cakes get eaten altogether?

- Use addition. Each lady has nine cakes so you can just add up six lots of nine cakes which is $9+9+9+9+9+9$ and comes to 54 cakes. A bit boring, you'll agree.

- You could try adding it up the other way round if you like. Suppose each lady eats one cake to start with – that's six cakes. Then they each eat another – which is six more. And so they kept going...

74

you'll get nine lots of six to work out which is
$6+6+6+6+6+6+6+6+6$ which also comes to
54 cakes and is even MORE boring.

- You can just zap it by using the tables: $6 \times 9 = 54$.
  If you prefer, you can zap it the other way round:
  $9 \times 6 = 54$. Whichever you choose, it's much neater,
  isn't it?

That was a multiplication sum, and if you know
the tables properly you can do the same sum backwards which is division.

75

There's six ladies running towards a pile of 54 cakes. How many can they each have? Let's do the sum with subtraction first:

Start with 54 cakes. Give each lady one – so that's six cakes less. How many cakes are left? $54 - 6 = 48$

You now have 48 cakes. Give each lady a second one – so you take six more cakes away. $48 - 6 = 42$

You now have 42 cakes. Give each lady a third... OH BOY, is this dull or what? We'll try something different.

Life is a lot simpler if you know your tables, because as soon as you see the number 54, a little bell will ring in your head.

From there it's just two sniffs and a wipe before you can say that the six ladies will get nine cakes each. As you can see, knowing the terrible tables is a pretty handy trick.

OK, we've put off the moment long enough. Here come...

The terrible times tables

	1	2	3	4	5	⑥	7	8	9	10
1	1	2	3	4	5	6	7	8	9	10
2	2	4	6	8	10	12	14	16	18	20
3	3	6	9	12	15	18	21	24	27	30
4	4	8	12	16	20	24	28	32	36	40
5	5	10	15	20	25	30	35	40	45	50
6	6	12	18	24	30	36	42	48	54	60
7	7	14	21	28	35	42	49	56	63	70
⑧	8	16	24	32	40	㊽	56	64	72	80
9	9	18	27	36	45	54	63	72	81	90
10	10	20	30	40	50	60	70	80	90	100

To find what any two numbers multiplied come to, you pick one of the numbers from the side and look along the row, and pick the other number from the top and look down the column to see where they meet. For instance to work out 8 × 6, you look along the "8" row and down the "6" column, and find the answer 48.

In all there are 100 numbers in the middle that

you have to learn, and if you want to bash it out, here's what you do:

Pick one of the numbers down the side, let's say "7". You then work along the row saying: "Seven times one is seven, seven times two is fourteen, seven times three is twenty-one..." and keep going until you get to "seven times ten is seventy". This is called "reciting the seven times table" and if you repeat it a few times, you'll soon remember it.

Although reciting the tables is the best way of learning how all the numbers slot in together, the trouble is that you just end up with a head full of figures which is no fun at all. It's a bit like looking at a photo of a crowd which is very boring...

...until you suddenly spot Frankenstein's monster and someone with two heads. As soon as a few people become interesting, then the whole photo starts to be much more entertaining. It's the same with the times tables, but how do we make some of the numbers interesting? The first thing to do is get RID of a lot of them. Hurrah!

We'll start by looking at the "1" on the top. As you look down the column, you'll see the numbers just go 1, 2, 3 and so on because if you multiply any number by 1 you just get the same number again. (You might think this is obvious, but it took the pure mathematicians thousands of years to decide sums like $7 \times 1 = 7$ were all right. No – don't laugh, that's cruel...)

Of course this also works with the "1" on the side, if you look along the row, again you just get 1, 2, 3. These are so simple, that we may as well make the table smaller by leaving all these out too.

Now look at the "10" on the top. As you look down the column, you'll see you just get 10, 20, 30 and so on. This is because of a very nifty arithmetrick which says that...

To multiply any number by 10, you move it all one place to the left and then plonk an extra 0 on the end.

Look at this:

$$
\begin{array}{r}
581 \\
\times \ \ 10 \\
\hline
= \underline{5810}
\end{array}
$$

See? This makes multiplying by tens very simple too, so we'll leave all the tens off the table.

By now we've decided that out of our 100 numbers, 36 of them are too simple to bother with, so let's see the table again:

	2	3	4	5	6	7	8	9
2	4	6	8	10	12	14	16	18
3	6	9	12	15	18	21	24	27
4	8	12	16	20	24	28	32	36
5	10	15	20	25	30	35	40	45
6	12	18	24	30	36	42	48	54
7	14	21	28	35	42	49	56	63
8	16	24	32	40	48	56	64	72
9	18	27	36	45	54	63	72	81

There, that's a bit better isn't it? We've only got 64 numbers left.

Just a minute though – if you look you'll start to see a lot of the numbers turn up TWICE. This is because multiplication can work either way round (i.e. 9×4 is the same as 4×9). There's no point in learning anything twice is there? No, so we'll get rid of another large chunk of numbers to make...

The terribly INTERESTING table

	2	3	4	5	6	7	8	9
2	4							
3	6	9						
4	8	12	16					
5	10	15	20	25				
6	12	18	24	30	36			
7	14	21	28	35	42	49		
8	16	24	32	40	48	56	64	
9	18	27	36	45	54	63	72	81

(YOU COULD RENT OUT THIS SPACE FOR ADVERTS)

Now then, let's see if we can find some of these numbers interesting. Maybe your birthday is on the 18th of the month. If you find 18 on the table you'll see that 18 is 3×6 (or 6×3 of course), so you could tell everybody it's the 3×6 of the month. With a bit of luck they might get confused and give you presents on the 3rd, the 6th AND the 18th. Nice one!

81

Another interesting number might be your house number. Suppose it's number 32. Imagine sending yourself a postcard with this on it:

DEAR ME
NOBODY UNDERSTANDS
HOW FABULOUS YOU ARE,
AND NOBODY APPRECIATES
HOW MUCH YOU SUFFER,
BUT I DO AND I LOVE YOU
LOTS AND LOTS!
        LOVE FROM ME xx

TO ME
8 × 4 GASWORKS
        LANE
POSHTOWN

The numbers coming down the sloping line of the interesting table are handy because they are called SQUARES. This is a way of saying they come from multiplying together two numbers that are the same, for instance 49 is 7×7 which is only half as hard to remember. You'll see that two of the squares also appear somewhere else on the table, so as well as being squares, they can be made using two different numbers. Can you see which two they are?

Here's some other interesting numbers. Pick any one of the squares. Move down one place and left one place. The number you get to is always one less! So if you start at 64 (which is 8×8), when you move down one and left one you get to 63 (which is 9×7). Let's call these "not quite squares".

Start with any of the "not quite squares" and again move down one place and left one place. The number you come to is always 3 less! (So if you start at 15, you'll end up on 12.)

Something else to do is colour in all the ODD numbers. (That is, any numbers ending in 1, 3, 5, 7 or 9). You'll see that a pattern appears.

By the time you've finished fiddling about with these numbers, you'll find that they all click into place and soon you'll feel like your head has been fitted with an automatic calculator. You'll be able to do simple multiplications and divisions in your head, but most importantly you'll be ready to play…

Assassins

Here's a merry little game for two people, the object being to assassinate the other person.

What you need:
● Ten little bits of paper each.
● 40 playing cards – one of you has the ace–10 of spades and clubs, the other has the ace–10 of diamonds and hearts.

How to play:
● Write a different number (between 1 and 100) on each of your slips of paper. Don't let the other person see your numbers.
● Both players look at their playing cards, pick one out and put it face down on the table.
● When you are both ready, turn the cards over and multiply the numbers together. If you have the answer on one of your bits of paper then POW! you have scored a hit. (So if your chosen card is a 7 and the other person picked a 3, and you had "21" on one of your bits of paper, then you would score a hit.)

- If you score a hit, you throw away the bit of paper, but for extra danger and excitement you can roll it into a little ball and ping it at the other person.

- Leave the playing cards on the table, and both choose another card to put face down.
- When you are both ready again, turn over the new cards and multiply the numbers together. Again, if you have the answer you score a hit.
- If you score three hits, then the other person is assassinated and you are the winner.

- If you run out of playing cards before anyone scores three hits, then it's a draw.

The tricks of the game:

1 Pick ten numbers that appear in the tables. The best numbers to pick are those that appear the most often.
2 When you pick a card to play, try to make sure it divides into at least one of your chosen numbers.
3 Try and remember what cards the other person has already played – it will help you choose what cards to play yourself. With a bit of practice you will learn how to "out-think" the other person.

A tables calculator – if you're utterly desperate!

Here's a way of multiplying two numbers together if you can't remember what the answer should be and can't think of any other way of working it out.

Suppose your sum is 4 × 7.

- Draw four lines going across.
- Draw seven lines running up and down. Each line must cross all four of the first lines.
- Count the number of places where the lines cross – and that's the answer!

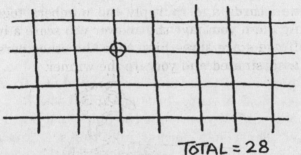

TOTAL = 28

The head-stretching trick!

Once you've sorted out the tables from 1–10, you'd be surprised at some of the bigger numbers you can quickly deal with in your head! How about this sum: 200 × 9,000?

THIS IS FAR TOO BIG TO FIT IN MY HEAD!

Relax! It's a very simple trick...

> **Multiply the two digits at the front, then count up the zeros and put them on the end!**

In this case all you do is work out 2×9, which you know from the tables is 18. You then count up all the zeros in the sum (and here we've got five of them) and write them afterwards. BINGO! the answer is 1,800,000. You'll see we've just put the commas in to make the answer look a bit tidier and us a bit cleverer.

Here's another: $800 \times 50,000$ comes to 40,000,000. What happened here is that 8×5 is 40, and then it gets another six zeros on the end because that's how many there were in the original sum. Of course the "40" we got also had a zero and that's why we ended up with seven zeros altogether.

Oh gosh – it looks like you've found out about the tables just in time because this book has been sabotaged! Did you notice the black spot on the last page? That isn't normal ink, that's a knock-out sleeping potion and when you read the page you accidentally put your thumb on it. A few deadly molecules have managed to seep through your skin and into your bloodstream and although you haven't realized it, you are now FAST ASLEEP and about to face an utterly diabolical challenge...

The morphing maze

"Where am I?" you groan as you open your eyes.

"Har har!" comes a voice. "You thought you were so clever escaping my scorpion trap, didn't you? Well this time I've really got you!"

Oh no, it's Professor Fiendish again with a massive bandage on his nose. You look around and see you are in a passageway with a large number nine painted on the floor in front of you.

HAR HAR!

Obviously the professor has gone to quite a lot of trouble painting it, so being a polite sort of person you make pleasant conversation.

"What's the big nine for?" you ask politely.

"You cannot pass over it without dividing yourself into the nine and morphing into another number," said the professor.

"What the great big frilly pants are you wittering on about?" you respond less politely.

"Har har! Look!" he says triumphantly, and holds up a mirror.

Gosh! Your whole body has been replaced by a large number 1.

"To get down the passage you must divide yourself into the 9 and see what you turn into!" laughs the professor.

"So here I'm dividing nine by one, so I just get nine," you say as you step across the wet paint.

ZAP! Your body morphs into a figure 9! This is pretty weird, even by the professor's standards. You look around and see three other passages leading away, each with a number painted on the floor.

"You can only pass over numbers that you can divide exactly into," chuckles the professor. "And when you have passed over, you turn into the answer!"

You see a number 72 on the floor and step over it.

ZAP! Your body turns from a 9 into an 8. (You remember the tables and realize this is because $9 \times 8 = 72$.) You step back and ZAP! Your body becomes a 9 again.

There is an 81 which you step over. ZAP you become another 9. Of course – that's because $9 \times 9 = 81$. You step back and ZAP, you are still a 9.

Just round a corner you see a 64 which you try and step over.

KERCHANGG! A massive metal spike shoots out of the floor and just misses you.

"Har har!" says the professor. "Nine won't go into 64, so you can't pass over it."

"What's the point of all this?" you ask, hoping he doesn't start off with one of his naff "har har"s.

"Har har!" he laughs predictably. "The only way you can get your body back is to reach the bottle of antidote, but you'll only get there if you cross the numbers in this order!"

You see he is waving a slip of paper covered in numbers at you, but suddenly an icy draught whisks it away to a distant corner of this book.

"Oops!" giggles the Professor. "Silly me! Now you'll have to work the route out for yourself, but frankly I don't fancy your chances!"

Diabolical indeed! But maybe, just maybe, if you keep a cool head and use the tables, you can get right through the morphing maze and reach the antidote!

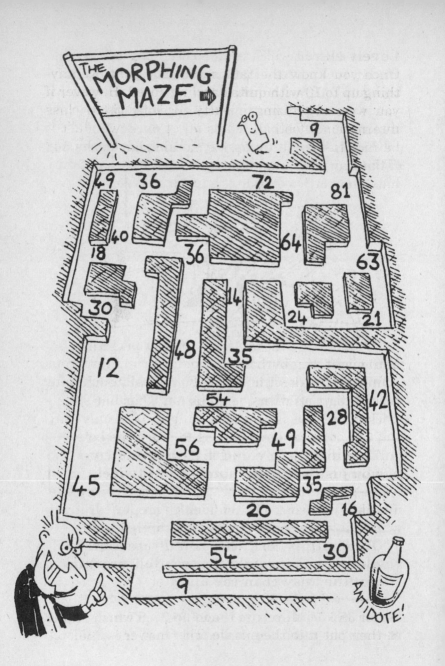

Lovely eleven

Once you know the tables you can multiply anything up to 10 with quite dazzling speed. However if
you were organizing a party for lots of top class
international football teams all at once, wouldn't it
be nice to have a quick way of multiplying by 11?
(That way you'd know how many crackers and funny
hats and bottles of orange squash to order.)

OI REF! HE'S
STEALING MY
CRISPS!

You might think that 11 would be a murderous
number to work with, but if you're dealing with one
or two digit numbers, there are a couple of simple
tricks...

**To multiply any one digit number by 11,
you just write the number out twice!**

In other words $8 \times 11 = 88$. Isn't that cute?

**To multiply any two digit number by
eleven, you just add the two digits up and
put the answer in the middle!**

So for 35×11 all you do is add up $3 + 5$ which makes
8, then put it in the middle. The answer is 385!

Aha! But does this trick work for any two digit number? How about 79? If you add up $7 + 9$ to get 16, then put 16 in the middle you get 7169, which looks a bit big! What you should do this time is put the 6 in the middle, but add the 1 on to the 7, so your sum comes out as $79 \times 11 = 869$.

So this trick will always work, even when you have a two digit number where the sum of the two numbers is also a two digit number (for instance $84 \times 11 = 924$).

MADDENING MULTIPLICATION

Although the tables only tell you how to multiply numbers from 1 to 10, you can use them to multiply any numbers you like. Look at this:

$$\begin{array}{r} 7 \\ \times\, 29 \\ \hline = \hphantom{00} \end{array}$$

Well the first trick to use here is that...

> **With multiplication, it's usually simpler to have the bigger number on top.**

Luckily when you're multiplying two numbers, you're allowed to swap them round without the world coming to an end so let's have this instead:

$$\begin{array}{r} 29 \\ \times\ \ 7 \\ \hline = \hphantom{00} \end{array}$$

← A THRILLING GAP.

You'll see that one of our little gaps has appeared too, which you might or might not need depending on how good your memory is.

Off we go then – all we do is take the lower number and use it to work along the upper number starting with the units, then moving back along from right to left. First you get your 7 and times it by the 9, which as you know from the tables makes 63. This is the same as six tens and three units, so

93

you can write the 3 units down in the units place...

$$
\begin{array}{r}
29 \\
\times\ \ 7 \\
\hline
=\ \ 3 \\
\scriptstyle 6
\end{array}
$$

Just so you don't forget the six tens, you can write a little 6 in the gap. Next we work back along the top number to the 2 in the tens place. When we multiply 2×7 we get 14. Before we write anything down, we suddenly remember the six tens we got before which need adding on to the 14 tens we just got. $14 + 6 = 20$. This means we put a 0 in the tens column, and carry over a 2 to the hundreds. As there is nothing left on the top line to multiply, we can write the 2 in the answer box.

$$
\begin{array}{r}
29 \\
\times\ \ \ 7 \\
\hline
=\ 203 \\
\scriptstyle 6
\end{array}
$$

And that's it! Of course if you thought that was grim you could have added $29 + 29 + 29 + 29 + 29 + 29 + 29$ and got the same answer.

Although the long way of doing multiplications will never let you down, it's always fun to see if there's a short cut. In this case, think about the number 29. If you had 29 sheep, that would be the same as having 30 sheep, but with one sheep missing.

It's the same with sevens. 29 sevens is the same as 30 sevens, but with one seven missing. All you do is work out 30×7 which is 210 (this is one of those easy "head-stretcher" sums we already saw on page 87), then knock one seven off so you get $210 - 7 = 203$.

However, not all numbers are quite so manageable…

Phew! Thank goodness we were here, because when a nurse asks for help, we heroes of Murderous Maths are proud to do our bit. Brace yourself because it's a nasty dirty sum but together we'll crack it:

$$
\begin{array}{r}
12834 \quad \text{total number of people} \\
\times \quad 217 \quad \text{spots on each person} \\
\hline
= \quad \text{total number of spots all together}
\end{array}
$$

To work it out, there are four choices.

1 You can write out $12834 + 12834 + 12834 +$ and so on, 217 times and add them all up. This is not recommended.

2 You can learn your 217 times table right up to 217 times 12834. This is even LESS recommended.

3 You could eat a handful of raw slugs in custard. This won't give you the answer, but at least it's better than option 2.

4 You just use the nice little set of tables we've already learnt and do a bit of simple adding.

We'll assume you don't like raw slugs, and even if you do, as anyone knows custard spoils that nice squelchy taste and you lose that feeling of their little eye stalks wiggling past your tonsils, so we'll see how to do option **4** which just happens to be one of the neatest arithmetricks:

> **You can split multiplications into simple bits, then work them out in turn, and finally add them together to get the answer.**

Here's what happens. Take the smaller of your two numbers and split it up into units, tens, hundreds and so on. In this case the number 217 is made up of 200 + 10 + 7. All we need to do is multiply 12,834 by each of these bits in turn and then add the lot up.

Yes please.

Multiplying by hundreds
We've already found out the trick of multiplying by ten, but it's so good that we'll have it again…

> **To multiply any number by 10, you move it all one place to the left and then plonk an extra 0 on the end.**

Multiplying by hundreds is just as easy...

> **To multiply any number by 100, you move it all two places to the left and then plonk 00 on the end.**

You get the general idea – for instance if you want to multiply by 1,000, you move everything 3 places and put 000 on the end, and to multiply by 10,000 you move 4 places and put 0000 on, but you've already worked that out, haven't you? Of course you have, because you've realized that this all ties in with the head-stretching trick we learnt earlier.

HERE YOU ARE.

Thanks. While it's cooling we'll have a quick reminder of what we're working out, it's 12834×217. Right then.

First we multiply the 12834 by the 200, which is the same as multiplying by 2 and then using our "hundreds" trick of moving the answer along two places and putting 00 on the end.

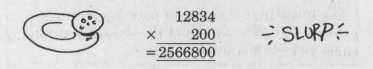

$$
\begin{array}{r}
12834 \\
\times \quad 200 \\
\hline
= 2566800
\end{array}
$$

≒ SLURP ≒

98

Now we multiply by the 10 which is easy peasy:

$$12834$$
$$\times \quad 10$$
$$= \underline{128340}$$

And finally we multiply by the 7:

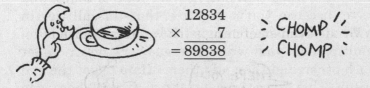

$$12834$$
$$\times \quad 7$$
$$= \underline{89838}$$

Now that we've done the little bits, we can add the three answers up.

```
   2566800   (This is 12834 × 200)
+  128340   (This is 12834 × 10)
+   89838   (This is 12834 × 7)
= 2784978   (And this is 12834 × 217)
```

And there's the final answer.

You'll see that there were four separate sums to get to the answer – three of them were multiplying sums and the last was an addition.

Instead of writing them all out separately, you can save time by writing them all out together like this:

$$
\begin{array}{r}
12834 \\
\times \quad 217 \\
\hline
2566800 \\
128340 \\
89838 \\
\hline
= 2784978
\end{array}
$$

What's happened here is that as you do each bit of multiplying, you write the answers down under each other, and then add them all up to get the end result. This saves time, but the main trick here is to make sure that all the numbers are lined up in the right place! Anyway, now we've finished let's hope we've helped in some way.

Other ways multiplication creeps up on you

A sum such as 27×9 can be described as...

- 27 times 9.
- 27 multiplied by 9.
- Multiply 27 by 9.
- Times 27 by 9.

But be careful because quite often it turns up heavily disguised...

- You could be asked to find the product of 27 and 9.
- Most of the time 27×9 would be called "twenty-seven nines" or "nine twenty-sevens".
- Even worse, if you are dealing with fractions, watch out for the word "of", because something like this: $\frac{1}{5} \times 40$ would usually be called "one-fifth of forty".

SOME MORE SNEAKY SIGNS

× TIMES

We already know what the "times" or multiplication sign means, but you do need to be a bit careful when you write it out. It should look like a little plus sign tipped over, but make sure it doesn't look like a letter "x" because in a lot of maths the letter "x" means "a mystery amount". Here's the trick of making sure you write them out differently:

One thing to watch out for: when maths gets complicated and people start using letters instead of numbers, quite often they leave the times sign out (so that $A \times B$ might be written as AB). Even more confusingly, they sometimes use a full stop instead of the times sign so that $A \times B$ becomes A.B but this is very irritating as it can look like a decimal point, and we'll find out about those later on. (Actually a decimal point appears in the middle of the line, not along the bottom like a full stop.)

Just like "+" and "−", the "×" sign is another operator and there is just one more main one that you need to know about:

÷ DIVIDED BY

In the same way that "minus" is the opposite of "plus", dividing is the opposite of multiplying, as we found out when we were messing about with the terrible tables.

102

Remember how we could move the numbers across to the other side in addition and subtraction equations? For instance we could turn $6 + 7 = 13$ into $6 = 13 - 7$ just by moving the "7" across and changing the sign from "$+$" to "$-$". With the very simplest multiplying and dividing sums (i.e. sums that don't include any addition or subtraction as well) you can do something similar. If we start with $8 \times 4 = 32$, we can move the $\times 4$ across and change the sign to $\div$ to get $8 = 32 \div 4$. This is all thanks to the old trick which is:

YOU MUST TREAT BOTH SIDES OF AN EQUATION EXACTLY THE SAME!

Thank you everybody. Right then, let's have a go with a $\times$ and $\div$ sum, and see if you can spot the SUBTLE DIFFERENCE in how it turns out compared to a $+$ and $-$ sum.

We'll start with...

$$7 \times 5 = 35$$

...and treating both sides the same we'll divide them both by 5.

$$7 \times 5 \div 5 = 35 \div 5$$

EVEN MORE NUMBERS FALL VICTIM TO CANCELLATIONS. READ ALL ABOUT IT!

$5 \div 5 = 1$

Here you'll see we have $\times 5$ and $\div 5$ next to each other which is *good news* because they cancel out and disappear completely. Let's see why...

Of course any number being divided by itself becomes 1, even $297 \div 297 = 1$ so it's time for another little cheer HOORAY and see what's left when we replace $5 \div 5$ with a 1.

$$7 \times 1 = 35 \div 5$$

Here's the good bit. We wouldn't usually bother putting "$\times 1$" in because multiplying anything by one doesn't change it, so we'll leave it out and look what we get:

$$7 = 35 \div 5$$

Just like we said: the "$\times 5 \div 5$" has disappeared! What's more the "$\times 5$" has swapped sides and changed to "$\div 5$".

Did you spot the subtle difference? With $+$ and $-$, when things cancel out you end up with 0 (for example $+324 - 324 = 0$) but with $\times$ and $\div$ when things cancel out you finish up with 1.

So what do you think of multiplying and dividing then? Things seems to cancel out happily enough, the equations don't look a lot different to the ones we had with addition and subtraction, in fact generally it doesn't seem too bad, does it?

Or are you slightly suspicious? Are you getting that kind of creepy feeling that comes when...

- You pick some socks off a shelf in the shop and realize they are just a little bit too warm and clammy?

- You bite into an apple and see half a worm wiggling out of the other bit?

- You sit down in the cinema and gradually realize that the seat is damp?

- You're having a bath in an empty house and see the door handle start to turn?

- You get a valentine card in November?

If you are getting that creepy feeling, then it's no wonder because dividing is where even the most innocent little numbers suddenly become murderous. Yes indeed, division is the gateway to mathematical hell, but we've come this far so there's no going back now. Get ready to hold your nose because we're going in...

DIABOLICAL DIVISION

Once upon a time there was a nice ordinary number 6. There she was skipping through a sunny field and picking daisies and not doing anybody any harm when she came across a jolly little 3.

"Do you want me to play with you?" asked the 3.

"Yes please!" said the 6, and so they played together nicely. First of all they played at adding...

$$6 + 3 = 9$$

...then they played at subtracting...

$$6 - 3 = 3$$

...then they had a go at multiplying...

$$6 \times 3 = 18$$

...and finally the 6 made a suggestion.

"How about doing some division?" she asked.

"Oh dear!" thought the little 3. His mummy had warned him about division, but that had made it sound all the more exciting. Maybe just one little game wouldn't hurt him!

"Well?" asked the 6. "Do you want to play division, or are you frightened?"

"I'm not frightened," gulped the 3. "Not frightened at all in fact."

"Good," said the 6. "Why don't you divide into me and we'll see what we get."

"How do we do that?" asked the 3.

"Simple," says the 6. "Just look for me on the tables and you will see that I can be made when a little 3 like yourself multiplies by 2. So if you divide into me, you will go two times like this..."

$$6 \div 3 = 2$$

"Brilliant!" said the 3. Just as he thought, his mummy had been making a big fuss about nothing.

WARNING

TO PEOPLE WITH A NERVOUS DISPOSITION: YOU MAY WISH TO CLOSE YOUR EYES WHILE YOU ARE READING THE NEXT FEW PAGES BECAUSE THEY ARE SO HORRID.!

As the 6 and the 3 sat and rested, along came a 7.

"You look like you are having fun!" said the 7. "Can I play too?"

"Of course," said the others, and they played a variety of games.

$$6 + 7 = 13 \qquad 7 - 3 = 4 \qquad 7 \times 6 = 42$$
$$3 \times 7 = 21 \qquad 3 + 7 = 10 \qquad 7 - 6 = 1$$

"That's enough kid's stuff," said the 7. "Now then, who's ready for a game of division?"

"ME!" cried the little 3.

"You're not scared then?" asked the 7.

"Of course not," replied the 3. "I'll divide into you, but how many times do I go?"

They looked at the tables.

"I only appear next to the 1 or another 7," said the 7. "Maybe I can't be divided by 3."

"That's silly!" said the 3. "Come on, we'll have a go anyway!"

So the 3 tried to divide into the 7.

$7 \div 3 = 2$ *and 1 left over*.

"Oh no!" said the 3. "I can't do it! I can go twice, but then there is one more left over, and I can't divide into that!"

"Let me try," said the 6.

$7 \div 6 = 1$ *and 1 left over*.

"Gosh!" said the 6. "I get one left over too!"

"Pathetic!" sneered the 7. "You're not doing it properly! Let me divide into you, I'll show you!"

$6 \div 7 =$ *but it wouldn't go!*

"See?" said the 6. "It's not that easy, is it?"

"You just wait," said the 7. "I'll try really hard this time."

And so the 7 tried as hard as he could.

He calculated, he carried over, he cancelled and suddenly there was an almighty explosion of decimals right across the field...

"Stop, stop!" screamed the 6. "You are reducing me into an infinite digital repetition of ever decreasing value!"

The 3 looked on in horror as he realized his mother had been right all the time. Sometimes division was safe enough, but most of the time it was murderous!

What's wrong with division?

So far we've just dealt with whole numbers such as 2, 17 and 56,893. Lots of things can only be counted in whole numbers such as how many coins you find down the back of the sofa, or how many goals are scored in a football or hockey match. As long as you only add, subtract or multiply whole numbers, your answer will always be another whole number. Sometimes you can be lucky with division and end up with whole numbers, but more often than not you are unlucky and you end up getting *fractions*.

Suppose you have been growing four clumps of hair on a big lump of old cheese and you decide it's time to share them out between three bald people.

Sharing is the same as dividing, so what we have is four clumps divided by three people which looks like this: $4 \div 3$.

To start with everybody can have one clump each...

...but there will be one clump left over. Of course, you can cut the last clump up into three equal clumpettes, and give each person a clumpette. This is the same as one divided by three, or written in numbers it's $1 \div 3$. But here's the question that's been rocking the mathematical world for centuries: how big is one hairy clumpette?

Here's where the dividing sign is interesting, because there's a neat little trick that shows what it's trying to tell you...

> **With dividing signs you can move the numbers on to the dots like this...**
>
> $1 \div 3$ $1 \div 3$ $\frac{1}{3}$

If you write one over three, you get a fraction called a "third" and in fact that is the official name for one divided by three, so if the last clump is shared between our three people, they will each get one-third of it. Don't forget that each person already had one whole clump to start with, so they each end up with $1\frac{1}{3}$ clumps of hair, and suddenly they all look terribly gorgeous because people with hair always do.

Please don't read this bit if easily offended...
As you know, the people at the *Murderous Maths* factory don't mind having a rude joke or two, but just occasionally things do get rather beyond their control. This is one of those occasions because right now we have to have a quick look at fractions, and

frankly if you are a sensitive person who is easily shocked, we suggest you close your eyes and block your ears before you read on.

There are two sorts of fractions, and we've already seen the first sort which have a number on the top (called a *numerator*) and a number on the bottom (called a *denominator*). It is fair to say that fractions like these are not exactly the cream of numerical society but with murderous maths we have to take the rough with the smooth, so just for a moment we'll brace ourselves and invite a few on to the page...

You see the problem? No wonder they are known as *vulgar fractions*. Of course the fault lies with division. If there was no such thing then we wouldn't have to tolerate this sort of low life fouling up the pages of this otherwise extremely high-class book.

Happily there is one way of avoiding vulgar fractions even if it is a bit desperate. You just feed them into a calculator.

In this case we'll just put $2 \div 7$ into the calculator and get...

The calculator has converted the vulgar fraction into a *decimal fraction* which isn't nearly as rude – but the trouble is that it's a real pain to do sums with. Later on we'll find out exactly how the calculator did this conversion, but in the meantime we'll banish fractions to a completely different book so that anybody who wants to avoid them can do so. (This book is called *The Mean and Vulgar Bits* and is not suitable for anyone who is easily offended or of a nervous disposition.)

When you can't have fractions
Sometimes when you divide you don't get nice whole numbers and you are not allowed to have a fraction either. You just end up with little spare numbers left over that you haven't a clue what to do with.

Suppose you have seven nice cuddly hamsters and you want to share them between four people. To start with each person can have one nice cuddly hamster each...

...but what do we do with the three nice cuddly hamsters remaining in the box? You can either do this:

THAT'S NOT FAIR ON ME.

Or this:

DO YOU WANT ME TO DIVIDE THEM UP FOR YOU?

BUT THEY WON'T BE SO CUDDLY THEN!

AND THAT'S NOT FAIR ON US!

As you can see, in this case there are a few hamsters left over that we can't do anything with, and anything left over tends to be called the *remainder*.

By now you will have realized that division is a nasty mean business, and so speaking of nasty mean things, it's time to introduce our very special guest star for this chapter. Yes, he's the man who put the OW into game show, will you please welcome Mr Titus O'Skinty!

Phew! Thank goodness he's given us an easy one to start with. Luckily for us we can find 21 on the tables, and we can see that it comes from 7×3. If $7 \times 3 = 21$ then $21 \div 3 = 7$.

Rats! If we're going to win anything we'll have to work a bit harder. A quick look at the tables tells us that 72 is the same as 8×9. This makes it easy if we wanted to divide by 8 or by 9, but that's no good because we want to divide by 4.

Yes, a lot of division sums do have short cuts, but if you can't spot a short cut then the only sure way to do any division is to work it out the long way. The first thing to do is write the sum out like this with a gap over the top where the answer will appear.

$$4\overline{)\,72}$$

With division you start by dividing into the left hand side of the number – so in this case you try and divide the four into the seven (which of course is seven tens because the seven is in the tens column). From the tables you know that four does not go into seven exactly, so you see what is the biggest number of times it could go. This turns out to be the same sum as when we were dividing the 7 hamsters by four kids, and the answer is that four into seven only goes ONE time, and there is a remainder left over. We write the ONE above the seven:

$$4\overline{)\,72}^{\,1}$$

118

Then we calculate what the remainder is. (Yes, obviously the remainder is three as we found out with the hamsters, but not all sums are as easy as this, so we'll take it slowly and see how we get there.)

What we do is multiply the one ten on top with the 4 and write the answer under the 72 and get this:

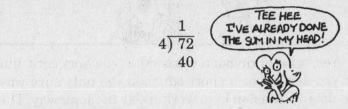

$$\begin{array}{r} 1 \\ 4\overline{)72} \\ 40 \end{array}$$

TEE HEE I'VE ALREADY DONE THE SUM IN MY HEAD!

What we will do now is see how much we have left out of our 72, so we take the 40 from it and get a remainder of 32.

$$\begin{array}{r} 1 \\ 4\overline{)72} \\ -40 \\ \hline 32 \end{array}$$

The next thing we are going to do is try and divide the 4 into 32, and when we look at the tables we see that UTTER JOY OF JOYS $32 = 8 \times 4$, so that means 4 goes into 32 eight times. We can write this 8 on the top in the units place.

$$\begin{array}{r} 18 \\ 4\overline{)72} \\ 40 \\ \hline 32 \end{array}$$

COME ON, COME ON WE'RE ALL WAITING.

In fact the answer to the sum has appeared on the top line: 18. However, just to make sure we have it right, it's a good idea to finish the calculation off. What we do is multiply the 8 we just put in the answer by our 4 and put the result at the bottom.

$$
\begin{array}{r}
18 \\
4\overline{)\,72} \\
40 \\
\overline{32} \\
-32 \\
\end{array}
$$

You then subtract the 32 we've just written down from the 32 that was there before to see if there is any remainder, and of course we get $32 - 32 = 0$. This means there is no remainder, and the calculation is complete.

If you wanted to check the answer, of course, you could multiply it all back up again by working out 18×4 and seeing if you get 72...

HURRY, HURRY, HURRY—
YOUR TIME IS NEARLY
UP!

...but we haven't time now so we'll just say the answer is 18.

SO ARE THEY RIGHT?

LET ME CHECK WITH MY SHORT CUT

This is starting to look mean! There's no 17 on the tables and certainly there is no 629. Mind you, it would be nice to win £100, wouldn't it?

Unfortunately the crow is right, you can't do division in easy bits like you can with multiplication. Gladys is right too, there's no short cut so we'll just have to smash through the whole thing at once! Actually it isn't too different from our 72 ÷ 4 sum earlier so let's get our heads down, but before we do we'll need a couple of naughty words. You can choose your own and write them in the boxes here:

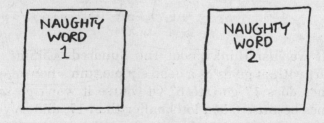

Have you filled in your naughty words? If you can't think of any, go and ask your granny for some. She'll probably pretend she doesn't know any, but then ask her if she would help you with some LONG DIVISION. You would be surprised how that can make even the sweetest old girl suddenly flare up and come out with a whole range of choice utterances.

Right then, off we go. First we write out the sum as before, leaving a space on top for the answer.

$$17) \overline{629}$$

There is a very special trick to help with these long division sums...

> **Long division sums involve a lot of GUESSING so it helps to use a pencil!**

The fun bit of long division is that we can make life a lot easier for ourselves. 629 is too big a number to think about all at once, so to start with we'll pretend we've covered the end of the sum up.

$$17) \overline{6}29$$

If we just think about the hundreds column to start with, it gives us a dead simple sum – how many times does 17 go into 6? Of course it won't go any times because 6 is a lot smaller than 17, and so you could write a 0 over the 6 to remind you if you like.

$$17\overline{)6\,29}$$
with a 0 above the 6

Actually most people wouldn't bother putting the 0 in, but it isn't such a silly idea because it does help you make sure that you write your next number in the correct place.

We now move along one place to include the tens column as well, and we divide 17 into 62. This is fun too, because we have to make a guess.

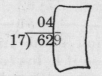

$$17\overline{)6\,29}$$
with 04 above

Let's guess that 17 goes into 62 four times, so we write a 4 in the tens column, then multiply this four by 17 which comes to 68 which we write in underneath.

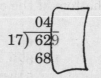

$$17\overline{)6\,29}$$
with 04 above and 68 underneath

We then take 68 from 62 to see what the remainder is... HANG ON! 68 is too big to take away from 62. It's time to shout out your first naughty word.

Ha ha! Serves him right. Anyway, now we know that our guess of 4 was too big, so we'll rub out the 4 and the 68 and try again with a smaller number. How about 3?

Hmm ... when we multiply the 3 by the 17 we get 51. Take that away from the 62 and we get 11 which is more like it. Now it's time to move along to include the 9 from the units column. All you have to do to bring the 9 in is "drop it down" to join the other numbers at the bottom of the calculation.

It's guessing time again – how many 17's go into 119? We'll try 6.

```
      036
17) 629
    51
    119
    102
     17
```

We then multiply 6 by 17 to get 102, take that away from 119 and get a remainder of... 17! That means that we could have divided one more 17 into 119.

Shout that second naughty word. Go on, you know you want to.

Wahey! Still, no time for laughing because we've nearly cracked it. We'll rub out the 6 in the answer and write 7, and when we change the sums we get this:

```
      037
17) 629
    51
    119
    119
     00
```

That's it! There's no remainder – we can say the answer is 37!

What do you think? Shall we play for the car? Why not? Let's face it we're getting pretty good at this dividing lark.

It looks like Gladys has seen another short cut, but as we don't know about factors, we'll just steam in and smash this sum to bits. It won't take long with our devastating combination of top tricks, bulging brains and heavenly good looks.

The calculations come out like this:

$$
\begin{array}{r}
48 \\
91\overline{)\ 4375} \\
-364 \\
\hline
735 \\
-\ 728 \\
\hline
7
\end{array}
$$

There's two things to notice here. The first is that 91 would not go into 4, then it would not go into 43, so our first guess was "how many times will 91 go into 437" and the answer was 4. It looks hard, but you'll find that making these guesses gets easier with practice!

The second thing to notice is that we have a little 7 left over at the bottom! This is because 91 will not go into 4375 exactly, instead it goes 48 times with a remainder of 7.

THEY HAVE AN ANSWER OF 48, TITUS, WHICH IS VERY CLOSE!

HAR HAR! BUT NOT CLOSE ENOUGH IF THEY WANT TO WIN THE CAR! SO WHAT ARE YOU GOING TO DO WITH THE EXTRA 7 THEN?

We can't let him beat us now! Remember when we divided the last hairy clump into three pieces? We got $\frac{1}{3}$. Here we are dividing the last 7 into 91 pieces, so maybe we can just write it like this: $\frac{7}{91}$.

Thank goodness Gladys knows how to deal with fractions, she must have read *The Mean and Vulgar Bits*. Anyway, we won't worry too much about what she did, the fact is that we've won the car!

What a swizz! But at least we got something and what's more, we've nearly found out how a calculator makes decimal fractions. That surprised you, didn't it?

Punishment for calculators

If you catch your calculator doing something naughty (for instance it might be chatting up the TV remote control) you can punish it by making it convert some vulgar fractions to decimals. Mind you, some fractions are easy to convert and others are harder, so let's see what's going on.

If we were going to work out a sum like $19 \div 8$, we would find 8 goes into 19 two times, and we'd have a remainder of three. As we are jolly sensible, we could write the answer like this: $2\frac{3}{8}$, and decide we've done enough. Calculators are not as clever as us for two reasons:

● calculators can't write vulgar fractions.
● calculators never know when to stop.

Sometimes you can make a calculator keep doing a division for ever, desperately hoping it will eventually come out. Here's how the sum for $19 \div 8$ would look if a calculator did it on paper:

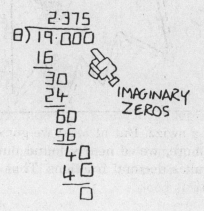

IMAGINARY ZEROS

When we did divisions, we had to keep moving along and bringing down the next digit until we had used them all up, and then if there was a remainder we just finished off with a neat little vulgar fraction. The calculator does the same thing, but if it still has a remainder when it has run out of digits, it starts bringing down imaginary zeros. At least it does do one sensible thing – as soon as it starts fantasizing and inventing these imaginary zeros to bring down, it puts a little dot in the answer, and this dot is called the ***decimal point***. In this case, the calculator has converted the $2\frac{3}{8}$ into a decimal which is 2·375.

As it turns out, the calculator was lucky here because after it had used the third imaginary zero there wasn't a remainder, so it could stop. In fact "eighths" are one of the easier fractions to put into decimals, but some fractions make your calculator break into a real sweat. Which of these do you think come out simply, and which will jam up the whole screen with digits?

If you've got a calculator you could try them out and see.

You'll find more about the decimal point and other signs that decimals use in "The sneakiest signs!" later in this book.

Other ways that division slithers into your life
Division is probably the sneakiest thing in maths
for suddenly turning up unexpectedly. If the sum
you have to work out is 56 ÷ 8, sometimes it turns up
obviously like this...
- 56 divided by 8
- 8 into 56
...but more often than not it it disguised by little
innocent phrases such as...
- 56 over 8
- how many times can you take 8 from 56?
- how many 8s are there in 56?
- how many 8s can you get out of 56?
- what is 56 shared by 8?
Don't be fooled – they are all the same sum!

Congratulations
You've now got through the toughest chapter in this
book, so you deserve a bit of a treat. Remember back
in the "cracking code" chapter we mentioned a
RUDE JOKE? Here it is...

THE RUDE JOKE

Question: What's invisible and smells of carrots?
Answer: 25 19 3 4 11 29 26 7 19 38 39

To decode the answer you need the KEY NUMBER which you have to work out by doing this sum: $37557 \div 39$. Don't go reaching for your calculator because that isn't going to help! We don't want any idiot who can prod a few buttons to know this great joke, it's only for people who can crack long divisions using their brains.

Start by writing it out like this:

$$39)\overline{\ 37557\ }$$

Do the whole sum the long way with all the working out right to the very end until you finish up with 0 at the bottom. You then count up how many times the digits 1 and 2 appear in your calculations and that is the key number!

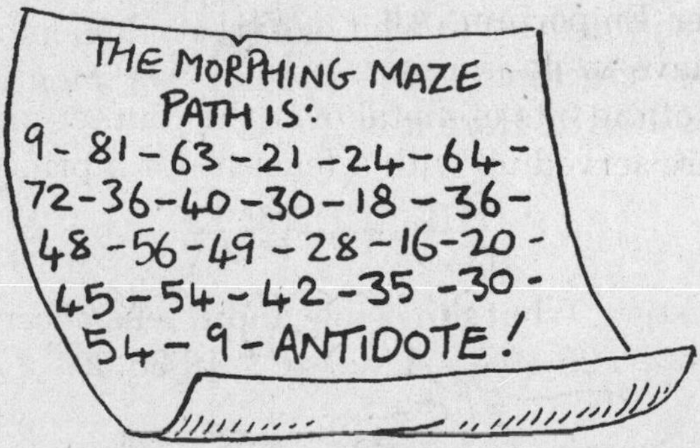

THE MORPHING MAZE PATH IS:
9 - 81 - 63 - 21 - 24 - 64 -
72 - 36 - 40 - 30 - 18 - 36 -
48 - 56 - 49 - 28 - 16 - 20 -
45 - 54 - 42 - 35 - 30 -
54 - 9 - ANTIDOTE!

SMALLER TROUSERS AND THE GOLDEN PROMISE

Once you've got the hang of the essential arithmetricks, one of the most useful things you can do with them is keep track of your money. By now you'll be able to work out how much a bagful of shopping should add up to and what change to expect when you pay for it, but if you think about it, money is amazing stuff.

For instance, there you are toddling along with a few bits of metal rattling about in your pocket, and suddenly you fancy a burger. Luckily you just happen to be passing Pongo McWhiffy's Deluxe Burger Emporium. All you have to do is pass  some of the bits of metal over the counter and there you are served up with a feast fit for a princess.

But why does Pongo think it's worth going to all the trouble of getting the ingredients, cooking them up and serving them to you just for some small bits of metal? He can't eat the bits of metal, he can't bang them into the wall and use them as nails, he can't write a letter on them or even thread them on to a string to make a necklace. They are utterly useless.

The answer is that these small bits of metal are MONEY and so they have the magic ability to turn into a burger or anything else (as long as it's fairly cheap). Of course there is also paper money such as £10 notes, and if you have enough of them you can turn them into a telly or something posh like that. Just about everybody on earth now uses some system involving coins and banknotes. Let's look at the whole story of money from start to finish and find out how it works.

The invention of money
As different kinds of money system gradually developed in different parts of the world, it's a bit unfair to give any particular bunch of people the credit for them, so here's a generalized version of what happened. We'll start many thousands of years ago with Udd and Blagga. Udd has three pterochicks and Blagga has a skinful of cowosaur milk.

Udd wants the milk and Blagga wants the chicks so they agree to swap. This arrangement works well, until a few thousand years later when Udd has forgotten to bring any pterochicks. Blagga refuses to hand over the milk, unless he gives her something else. Udd picks up a stone from the ground and offers it to Blagga. Blagga is not impressed because there are tons of stones around, so she could pick up as many as she wanted. However Udd is suddenly lucky because he finds a yellow shiny stone which is very unusual. Blagga is rather taken with it and agrees to hand over the milk for the yellow stone.

A few thousand years later on, people are quite happy to swap their apples, blankets, elephants or spears for these shiny yellow stones. Although a lot more yellow stones have been found, they are still quite rare which gives people the confidence to use them. (If they were all over the place, they'd be pretty but not valuable.) Udd now has a big hat, but what he really wants is a pogo stick. Blagga has a pogo stick, but the only thing she wants is to have her dung heap turned into a patio. Thanks to the yellow stones, this tricky deal can be arranged.

All Udd has to do is find somebody with a yellow

stone to spare who wants a big hat. Udd swaps his hat for a yellow stone, then goes to see Blagga. Blagga agrees to let him have the pogo stick in return for a yellow stone. Blagga can now give the yellow stone to the patio basher in return for his services!

One big advantage of the yellow stone system was that you didn't need to wear massive trousers. If you went out on a shopping spree, you just had to take a few yellow stones which would easily fit in your pocket. However, if Udd hadn't originally picked up the first yellow stone, then pockets and handbags would need to be radically bigger.

THAT'll BE TWO COWS, A BAIL OF STRAW AND SIX RHODODENDRON BUSHES PLEASE.

Yes, the yellow stone system was a great improvement but the next problem to overcome was that not all yellow stones were the same size. To make it fair, they wrote numbers on each yellow stone to say what size it was. The smallest yellow stones would just be worth "1", and bigger stones would be worth "2" or "3" or more.

Obviously a stone marked "3" would be worth the same as three stones marked "1". This was a better system, but sadly even in those days there were people who tried to cheat.

To make yourself richer, all you had to do was change the numbers on your stones! For instance you could rub off a "4", put on a "5" and with a bit of luck nobody would notice. It's hardly surprising then that the people in charge tried to stop this happening.

Luckily these shiny yellow stones had a magical property because when you heated them up they melted. This meant that you could make your stones an exact shape and size, and you could also stamp a complicated design on them so that people would find it harder to change them. In other words they made gold coins.

As one gold coin was worth quite a lot they also made coins from other metals such as silver and bronze which were worth less and soon a whole system was developed, for instance a hundred small bronze coins might be worth one silver coin, and a hundred silver coins might be worth one gold coin. This allowed you to use coins to buy anything from a cup of soup to an entire restaurant.

So far so good then, but what if you had a ton of gold coins and were stuck in your castle surrounded by Grizelda the Grisly and her evil hoard of bandits? It makes sense to hire Urgum the Axeman to turn up with his army and help you out. Of course, Urgum will want paying and he doesn't come cheap. The only answer seems to be to get a horse and cart and load it up with gold and send it to Urgum, but the chances are that Grizelda will hear it clinking down the path and pinch the lot. However there is a slim chance that you can still get Urgum without risking your money. What you do is write a note and send it by carrier pigeon. Here's the note:

Urgum knows all about your ton of gold coins, so when he gets the note he knows that you will be able to pay him. Clutching his bit of paper, he kicks his army out of bed and they all come charging at

Grizelda's Grislies. The scene is too horrible to describe to sensitive, intelligent Murderous Maths readers – so we'll leave it. Instead we'll concentrate on the interesting thing here, which is that instead of sending the gold to Urgum, you issued your very own bank note!

The golden promise
In England, all paper money has three important things printed on it:

- At the top it says "BANK OF ENGLAND".
- There is a statement saying "I promise to pay the bearer on demand the sum of..." and then underneath it says how much, e.g. ten pounds.
- Somewhere underneath the promise, the note is signed by the "chief cashier". (To be honest it's only a printed signature because the chief cashier is usually too busy having lunch or playing golf to sign all the notes personally.)

Does this mean that for every single banknote in circulation, the Bank of England has enough gold to pay everybody out? Sadly not. It *used* to be true, though, and in the 19th century lots of countries used a system called "the Gold Standard", which meant that you could take a massive wad of cash to the bank and get a gold bar for it. However, since the 1930s things have got a lot more complicated, and even though the promise is still on every banknote, the government doesn't have enough gold for them all. (Mind you, they still have quite a lot of gold which is called the "gold reserves".)

The reason the system still works is because countries still have to trade with each other. Trading is just a posh version of doing a "swap" (like when Udd swapped three chicks for Blagga's milk) and the more you've got to swap or trade with, then the better you're doing. International Money Markets such as Wall Street in New York or the City of London spend ages deciding the value of different countries' money, and to do this they take into account how much the different factories and farmers are producing to trade with. Sometimes countries have good years and at other times they have bad years and that's why if you take £10 on holiday abroad, some years it will get you more foreign money than others.

You'd think that if a government was feeling a bit poor and wanted to give all the members of parliament triple wages they could just print off a load more paper money, wouldn't you? Sometimes governments do print more money than the country is really worth, but it gets them into very serious trouble. As soon as the International Money Markets know they are cheating, the value of the country's money drops and it can end up completely unable to trade or do deals. The next thing you know the government's heads are all stuck on poles for crows to peck at. Serves them right too.

Incidentally this is also why "counterfeiters" (i.e. people who make fake money) are so dangerous. You might think there is not much harm in running off a few dud twenties, but as soon as people lose confidence in these bits of paper that we buy things with, the whole system can collapse. In wartime, enemy countries often try to forge each other's money because it can cause so much damage. Luckily it is very rare that anybody dares to cheat the system, so we are all confident that banknotes are worth something. These days we've taken things a step further – you don't even have to hand over notes or coins, you can just wave a plastic credit card about (as long as you're old enough).

What happened to coins?
Originally coins were made of gold or silver, and so they were valuable items in themselves. Of course these days coins are made of all sorts of cheaper metals, but they are now doing a different job. Suppose we didn't have coins, instead we just had banknotes which went right down to values like 1p

and 2p. You'd end up with a lot of irritating scraps of paper to count out and keep track of, so instead we have bits of metal to represent small amounts. Of course if you save up your bits of metal, you can afford to swap them for a paper banknote.

There are a few rare exceptions, one of which is the South African Krugerrand. This is a *real* gold coin, so if you ever get one, don't put in a drinks machine by mistake!

Whether you use metal coins, paper banknotes or plastic credit cards, the money system we use today is pretty much the same system as Udd and Blagga all those years ago. If money hadn't been invented and you wanted a burger, there would only be one thing for it...

WHEN NOTHING MEANS SOMETHING

Prepare to meet a quite amazing man:

DID YOU KNOW THAT THERE'S 31,682 FLIES IN MY COW SHED?

See? How many other people do you know that would bother to count all their flies right down to the last one? To put it kindly, this guy is definitely one teat short of an udder.

THAT'S NOTHING, I'VE GOT 42,000 DUNG BEETLES IN MY PIG STY.

Now that's more like it. Does this lady mean that there are exactly 42,000 dung beetles in her pigsty? Of course not, she has had the sense just to give us a rough answer which was accurate to two *significant digits*. (Or you can call them *significant figures* if you really want to. Go on you crazy groover, do your own thing.) In other words she only bothered telling us the first two numbers exactly, then finished her number off with zeros. It was enough to give us the general idea of what the inside of her pigsty was like, and let's face it the less we know about that the better.

With any long numbers, the digits that come at the front are always more important (or more "significant") than those that come at the end. If you have seven million and nine pounds in the bank, then who cares about the £9, when you've got a great big fat £7,000,000 as well? That's why with long numbers, the digits at the end usually get made into zeros to make life simpler.

Significant digits are the digits in a number before the zeros start. Let's see a few examples:

THERE ARE 3,100 TADPOLES IN MY POND.

Urgh!   (2 SIGNIFICANT DIGITS)

I'VE GOT 58,320 ROTTEN EGGS IN MY BARN.

Pooh!   (4 SIGNIFICANT DIGITS)

Where?

Because the zeros don't count as significant digits, you might think they don't mean anything, but in fact they do a very important job. Look at the numbers 561 and 561,000 – obviously they are not worth the same even though both numbers have the same three significant digits. The zeros tell us what the digits are worth, whether it's thousands, millions, hundreds or even tenths, hundredths, thousandths, millionths, etc!

LOOK AT THIS. 0·0000561

Yes, you also find significant digits in decimal fractions, and as you can see this fraction has the same three significant digits. With decimal fractions the zeros come between the point and the first significant digit.

How to tidy up nasty numbers

If you have a long complicated number and want to make it look nicer, all you need to do is choose how many significant digits you want to bother with, and then round the rest of the number off. To see how "rounding off" works, let's grab a long number:

853,619

Gotcha! Now lie still because we're going to round you off.

- Suppose we only want two significant digits, this number will round off to 850,000. This is because the number 853,619 is somewhere between 850,000 and 860,000 and the trick is to choose which of these numbers is closer. In this case it is 850,000.

- If we want three significant digits then it would round off to 854,000. You might be surprised that a 4 turned up instead of the 3, but remember that we want to keep the new number as close as possible to the old one. If you think about it, 854,000 is closer to 853,619 than 853,000 is.

There is a trick to help you get rounding off right...

If the next digit is a five or bigger, then add one to the last significant digit.

This is such an important trick, you'll find it disguises itself and sneaks into every single *Murderous Maths* book! In this case, when we rounded 853,619 off to three digits, the next significant digit would have been a 6. That's why the 3 got "rounded up" to a 4.

Here are some numbers rounded off to four significant digits, with a bit of commentary to keep you company while you're admiring how lovely they all are.

- 35,817 → 35,820

  Nice and easy, the 7 means that the 1 rounds up to a 2.

- 0·000687593 → 0·0006876

  Again it's easy. When the 9 and the 3 go, don't bother putting any zeros in their place because after the decimal point, zeros at the end don't mean anything. (Well actually they do as you'll see in a minute, but in this case it would be wrong to put them in.)

- 273 → 273

  Extremely easy. As you only have three significant digits to start with, there's nothing to round off.

- 12·3248 → 12·32

  Very hard this one. No, only kidding. Of course it's dead easy. Don't be worried by where the decimal point is, just make sure you keep it in the same place.

- 13,071 → 13,070

  This is a bit exciting, because the zero in the middle is actually one of the four significant digits, even though it is a zero.

- 369,981 → 370,000

  What happened here is that because the next digit is an 8 we added 1 to the last 9 of the first four digits. Of course what we are really doing is

149

adding 1 to 3699 and that's how it got to be 3700. The funny thing about the answer 370,000 is that the first two zeros are significant and the last two are just plain old insignificant zeros! Look pretty much the same, don't they?

When zeros are significant

If somebody says their dog has 2,800 fleas, then you would presume that they meant "around" 2,800 fleas. You would also presume that the zeros were not significant, but the 2 and 8 were. With the way rounding up or down works, that means the dog could have as many as 2,849 fleas or as few as 2,750. There is a difference of 99 between the smallest possible number and the largest! That's a lot of fleas.

However if you were told it was 2,800 fleas, *and the number was accurate to three significant digits*, then that means the 2, the 8 and the first 0 are significant. In this case the dog could have as many as 2,804 fleas, or as few as 2,795. This time there is only a difference of 9 between the smallest number and the largest. Obviously, when a zero is significant, it makes a big difference!

IT DOESN'T MAKE THAT MUCH DIFFERENCE TO ME!

With normal numbers, you don't know a zero is significant unless somebody tells you, but with decimal fractions there is a way of telling.

If you round off 0·01781 to two significant places, you get 0·018.

However if you round off 0·02961 to two significant places you might be tempted to put 0·03 and leave all the zeros at the end out. This is sad because if you think about it, you've only shown one significant digit (the 3) and left it at that. In fact your number is more accurate than that, and so to show it's accurate to two significant digits, it makes sense to put a zero *after* the 3. That way, if somebody sees the fraction 0·030, they will know it is accurate to two significant digits and they will love you all the more for it.

There's one little trick to bear in mind...

> **Once you have rounded a number off, don't bother being too accurate with it again.**

This rather good joke explains why:

151

(Interestingly, this joke is about the same age as the dinosaur.)

How many digits do you need to worry about?
Sometimes you get told how many digits you need, but if there's nobody else sticking their nose in then it's up to you. As a general rule the trick is...

> **If you want to be fairly accurate without being boring, then two significant digits are enough, although if the first digit is a 1 it's better to give three.**

Sometimes, calculators can be a real pain – they love showing off by giving ridiculously complicated answers. If your calculator comes up with a number like 249·89537, you can have a good laugh annoying it by just rounding it off to 250.

Life is even more fun if you are doing some rough sums because one significant digit is usually enough, although if your first digit is a 1 or even a 2 then you should try and work with two digits. Gosh! What's a rough sum? It's probably the handiest thing you'll find out from this book, so let's hurry up and find out...

ROUGH SUMS AND GOING MENTAL

It's a tough old world in the pop business. Groups come and go so fast that sometimes there isn't time to mess about doing sums. In this case the theatre manager has had to make an instant decision – but was he being cheated or not? The fastest way to find out is to do a ***rough sum***. All you do is make the numbers involved as simple as possible, then you can quickly work out a rough answer.

In this case there are 25,373 tickets that cost £19 each and the manager is expecting half of that money. If you want to work out exactly how much money he should get, you calculate $25,373 \times 19 \times \frac{1}{2}$. This is a bit of a tedious sum, so to get a rough answer, you just change the numbers a bit like this:

- You could decide that 25,373 isn't too far away from 25,000, and 19 is very close to 20. You then work out that the number of pounds the manager expects to get is roughly $25,000 \times 20 \times \frac{1}{2}$. Of course half of 20 is 10, so the manager should be expecting roughly $25,000 \times 10$ which comes to £250,000.

If the manager had used a rough sum, it would only have taken him a few seconds to realize that the agent was stitching him up like a kipper.

154

There are no fixed rules to doing rough sums, it's just something that comes with practice. The main trick is...

> **Try to get as many zeros into your numbers as possible.**

This is because tens, hundreds and thousands are so easy to add, subtract, multiply and divide. Of course the way to get zeros into your sums is to use only one or two significant digits for each number as we found out in the last chapter. Once you have got a few zeros in, rough sums are a complete doddle.

Rough adding

I'VE GOT 2,346 BUCKS.

HERE'S 3,988 BUCKS.

I'VE JUST GOT 332 BUCKS

THERE'S 5,024 IN HERE. SO WHAT DID WE PULL ALTOGETHER?

Here's the sum:

```
    2346
    3988
     332
  + 5024
```

There are two ways to get a rough answer. You could round the numbers off to two digits and get $2,300 + 4,000 + 300 + 5,000 = 11,600$ which isn't too hard. An even rougher but faster way is to just add up the first two columns – in other words the hundreds and thousands. You get $23 + 39 + 3 + 50 = 115$, so roughly 11,500. Here you actually ignored all the tens and units and rounded the numbers down, so your answer will be a bit low, but as long as you know that, you can say:

Rough subtracting

156

Here's the sum:

$$11690$$
$$-2471$$

No problems! You can round the numbers off to get $11,700 - 2,500$ which gives an answer of about 9,200. You could have even rounded the numbers off more roughly to get $12,000 - 2,000$ which gives 10,000. But when you are rounding numbers very roughly, there are a couple of useful tricks...

For adding or multiplying two numbers very roughly, round one up and the other one down.

For subtracting or dividing two numbers very roughly, round them both up or round them both down.

In this case we are subtracting, so we round both numbers up and get $12,000 - 3,000$ which gives us an answer of about 9,000. This will turn out to be closer than the 10,000 we got before...

Rough times

LET'S CELEBRATE WITH OUR FAVOURITE FOOD! HOW MANY BREADSTICKS CAN WE BUY?

YOU CAN BUY 173 FOR $1, AND WE HAVE $9,219.

Here's the sum:

$$9219$$
$$\times 173$$

We'll work it very roughly, and the first trick to play with big multiplications is simply to cross some of the insignificant digits off (but we must keep count of how many we do cross off!) Let's make the sum into this:

$$92$$
$$\times 17$$

We've crossed off two numbers from the top line and one from the bottom, so that makes three crossed off numbers altogether. Write a big 3 on your nose or somewhere so you don't forget.

Now then, as it's a multiplication, remember the trick to round one number up and the other down.

Be careful here though, because if you round 17 right down to 10, you are making a big difference – you've almost chopped it in half! You would be better rounding the 17 up to 20 and the 92 down to 90 which gives an answer of $20 \times 90 = 1,800$. The other thing you could do is round the 92 up to 100 (which is a really nice rough number to work with) and just round the 17 down to 15 (which isn't too bad a number to work with). This gives $15 \times 100 = 1,500$. So which answer do you think is closer 1,800 or 1,500? Either of them are quite good, but just for fun let's pick a number in between the two: 1,600.

WHY HAVE I GOT A 'THREE' ON MY NOSE?

Gosh, well remembered! It's so we don't forget how many numbers we crossed off. What we have to do is put a zero on to our final answer for every number we crossed off. As we crossed off three numbers, we write on three zeros to get a final rough answer of 1,600,000.

YOU'll GET ABOUT 1,600,000 BREADSTICKS.

HOW DOES HE DO IT SO FAST?

I MAKE IT 1,594,887.

159

Rough division

As there are about 365 days in a year, here's the sum:

$$365 \overline{) 6212}$$

As it's a division, we round both numbers up or both down, so let's make it into:

$$400 \overline{) 7000}$$

Once we have a few zeros in place, the next thing we can do is cross some of them off. Division is different from multiplication in that we have to make sure we cross off the same number of zeros from both numbers. Here we can cross off two zeros each to leave us with:

$$4\overline{)\,70}$$

HAVE I GOT TO WRITE ANYTHING ON MY NOSE?

No, not with division, just as long as you cross the same number of zeros off from each number. If one of your numbers is too small then you can't cross any zeros off which is irritating, but then that's life isn't it?

Right then, we can't make this much simpler so let's hit it...

$$
\begin{array}{r}
17 \\
4\overline{)\,70} \\
\underline{4} \\
30 \\
\underline{28} \\
2
\end{array}
$$

We've got a remainder of 2 but who cares? This is only a rough sum so ignore it and proudly announce your answer...

Really very rough sums indeed

Some sums are so rough that you only need to work out the first significant digit and then the number of zeros involved. When you give *really* rough answers, you don't say the answer is rough, you say it is "in the order of".

For instance the distance from Earth to the sun is in the order of 100,000,000 miles. If you want to calculate how many miles it is from the sun to the next nearest star you need to know that...

- One light-year is 5,900,000,000,000 miles.
- The nearest star is 4·3 light-years away.

To get the answer we have to multiply these numbers together but to start with we'll rough it up. We'll say the light-year is about "6" with 12 zeros after it. Ignore the zeros for the moment, but remember there are twelve of them. The nearest star we'll say is 4 light-years away.

$4 \times 6 = 24$ and when we put the 12 zeros back on we can say that the distance from the sun to the next nearest star is in the order of 24,000,000,000,000 miles. If anybody thinks you're too far out, just tell them to go and measure it. That'll keep them quiet.

162

THE SNEAKIEST SIGNS!

We've already met quite a few signs, and here's some more starting with a few that help out with decimal fractions:

· THE DECIMAL POINT

This is that tiny little dot that separates whole numbers from decimal fractions. It's just like a full stop which has floated up a bit. If you offer to carry some shopping that weighs 1·457 kg, make sure that decimal point is clear! If the decimal point looks like a comma, then it could be murderous!

0·41$\bar{6}$ A LINE OVER A DECIMAL DIGIT

The line over the last digit of a decimal fraction means that this same digit is repeated for ever.

If you convert $\frac{5}{6}$ into a decimal fraction properly you get 0·83333333... and the threes would go all the way to Mars and back, and that's just for starters. Calculators try and write out as many threes as they can but as humans are more sensible we don't bother writing out more than we have to. You can put a line over the first 3 and leave the others off: 0·8$\bar{3}$ (or you could use a little dash like this: 0·8$\dot{3}$).

0·$\overline{571428}$ A LINE OVER A FEW DECIMAL DIGITS

Some decimal fractions have a set of digits that repeat for ever. If you work out $4 \div 7$ you would get 0·571428571428571428... and the digits would keep repeating all the way to Mars and bump into the threes coming back the other way. Putting a line over the top shows that the same pattern repeats without you having to spend the next million trillion years writing it all out, so it saves quite a bit of time, this sign, doesn't it?

NOW HE TELLS ME.

25·87345... DOTS AFTER DECIMAL DIGITS

This means that the digits go on for ever, but not in any particular pattern. Numbers that have this are called "irrational" because there is no way of writing them down absolutely exactly! In a minute we're going to see what "square roots" are, and most of them are irrational.

> GREATER THAN

This one is a bit like an equals sign. If you have $4 = 2 + 2$, then that says that "four equals two plus two". If you have $5 > 2 + 2$, that says "five is greater than two plus two". This sign often comes in computer instructions, for instance if a car park can only hold 100 cars, the computer could have an instruction programmed into it that says "If the number of cars > 100 then light up the car park full sign."

≥ GREATER THAN OR EQUAL TO

This speaks for itself really. Suppose you're having a spelling test and you have to get at least 5 out of 10 to pass. You score must be ≥5. You could also say your score must be >4.

HEY! WHY DON'T YOU PICK ON SOMEONE ≥ YOUR OWN SIZE?

< LESS THAN

Obviously this is the opposite of greater than, and it used to get used in the olden days after particularly nasty battles. "If the number of heads you have is <1 then you've had it."

≤ MYSTERY SIGN

Gosh, what could this mean, eh? A lot of books would give you the answer, but this one thinks you're intelligent enough to work it out for yourself. If you can't work it out then your number of brain cells must be ≤0.

% PER CENT

Often people use the per cent sign when they can't be bothered to use fractions or decimals. It means "out of 100" or "over 100", so if you have 50%, then that means $\frac{50}{100}$. If you wanted you could divide top and bottom by 50 and so make 50% into $\frac{1}{2}$. It means the same thing. Percentages are also very easy to write in decimals, you just put the number behind the decimal point so 50% is the same as 0·5. Watch out for very small percentages though – if the percentage only has a single digit such as 3%, you have to put a zero in front like this: 3% = 0·03.

! FACTORIAL

This sign usually means that you've just read something funny or amazing, and when you see it in a book or a comic, it is called an exclamation mark. However in maths it means something completely different – in fact it is rather exciting because it is an OPERATOR. Unlike other operators it can only go with whole numbers, and it gets written in immediately afterwards like this: 11! Here it means $11 \times 10 \times 9 \times 8 \times 7 \times 6 \times 5 \times 4 \times 3 \times 2 \times 1$. So in other words the ! tells you to multiply the number by every other number smaller than it right down to 1.

Factorials are especially useful in working out "permutations and combinations". Suppose you are writing a pop song, and you want the words "Hey" "Groovy" "Baby" "Yeah" in the title, how many ways are there of mixing them up?

For instance you could have "Groovy Baby Yeah Hey" or "Baby Hey Yeah Groovy" or even "Hey Yeah Baby Groovy". Because you have four different words to play with, the answer is that there are 4! ways. You can test this – first of all try writing out all the combinations of "Hey" "Groovy" "Baby" and "Yeah" that you can, then work out $4 \times 3 \times 2 \times 1$. After you've done that, you can throw open the window and sing your song as loudly as you can down the street. It might not be maths, but it would certainly be murderous.

Factorials are also really useful in working out the laws of chance. This is when you work out how likely it is that you'll win a dice game, or whether a seagull will splatter you at the seaside.

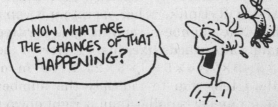

Chance is one of the most fun (not to mention most murderous) bits of maths, so if you should happen to see a book called *Do You Feel Lucky?*, make sure you treat yourself to it.

( ) BRACKETS

When you are solving a complicated sum, you can't do it all at once. The trick is to work out the various bits in the right order.

First calculate the things in brackets.

Then do any other multiplying or dividing.

Finally do any adding or subtracting.

Look at this: $3 \times (2+7) - (4+8) \div (4-2)$

Do the bits in brackets first and you get $3 \times 9 - 12 \div 2$. Then do the multiplying and dividing and get $27 - 6$. Finally do any adding or subtracting and get the answer 21.

If the brackets were not there we would have had $3 \times 2 + 7 - 4 + 8 \div 4 - 2$. Doing the multiplying and dividing would give us $6 + 7 - 4 + 2 - 2$. And the answer would have been 9. As you can see, the brackets make a lot of difference!

2 SQUARES, CUBES AND OTHER POWERS

Very often in maths you have to multiply a number by itself, and you can describe this in lots of ways. If you have 4×4 you can call it...

- the square of 4
- 4 to the power of 2
- or using numbers you write it with a cute little 2 in the corner like this: 4^2.

Whatever you do, 4 squared comes out to 16. (You might remember that this was one of the "squares" we met when we looked at the terrible tables.)

"Cubes" are when you multiply a number by itself three times, so 5 cubed is the same as 5 to the power of 3, which is $5 \times 5 \times 5$ or 5^3 and comes to 125. (Don't get cubes confused with multiplying 5 by 3 which just makes 15. There's a big difference!)

This works for raising a number to any power. "7 to the power of 6" is the same as 7^6 which is $7 \times 7 \times 7 \times 7 \times 7 \times 7$ and comes to 117,649.

You can even have powers of powers such as 2^{3^2}. If you work out the 3^2 bit, that comes to 3×3 which is 9, so your number is really 2^9 which works out at 512.

Pure mathematicians even use powers of powers of powers to describe absolutely ridiculous numbers such as: $10^{10^{10^{34}}}$ which is ten to the ten to the ten to the thirty-four. This one is known as Skewes's number and works out to be quite a lot. When you get much higher than this then some numbers start to go a bit peculiar and the whole fabric of maths starts to fall apart.

It's like the equivalent of "meltdown" in a nuclear power plant, and you don't want to be picnicking too close to it.

$\sqrt{}$ SQUARE ROOTS

These are the opposite of squares. You start off with a number, and you have to find a number which when you multiply it by itself gives the number you started with. Suppose you start with 9, the square root of 9 is 3 because $3 \times 3 = 9$. You can also write it like this $\sqrt{9} = 3$.

Unless you have a calculator with a $\sqrt{}$ button, most square roots can be murderous to work out. Even our nice number 12 has a square root that comes out to 3·46410161514... and as you can see from the dots, it is irrational.

Even worse are "cube roots" which means you start with a number and try and find a number that when cubed comes to the first number. Because $4^3 = 64$, we can write $\sqrt[3]{64} = 4$ but to work out most cube roots you'll need a really good calculator with a fancy button on it that probably looks like this $x\sqrt{}$

Just out of interest, if you prefer you can write out roots with little fractions like this:

$$\sqrt{25} = 25^{\frac{1}{2}} = 5 \quad {}^{3}\sqrt{216} = 216^{\frac{1}{3}} = 6$$

By now you might be starting to worry that all this is getting a bit too murderous, so we'll just look at one last sign which is made up of three letters:

QED

This is the most satisfying thing to write in maths! You use this when you've been trying to prove something and you think you've done it. To demonstrate, let's snoop on another touching encounter between Pongo McWhiffy and the terribly lovely Veronica Gumfloss.

Actually QED comes from Latin and stands for "Quod Erat Demonstrandum" which means "that which was to be demonstrated". But when you've been bashing away for days on some meganormous calculation and finally write QED what you're really thinking is "Quite Enough Done". Once you've written QED then it's time to have a big sigh, slip off your shoes, lie back, pull your shirt up and have a little game of flicking paper pellets into your belly button. Bliss.

THE FIENDISH FORMULA!

"Har har!" cackles an all too familiar voice. "So you think you know all about equations and signs and sums now do you?"

Good grief! In one final desperate attempt to defeat you, Professor Fiendish has just produced his most diabolical device yet – the Fiendish Formula.

"You'll see there are eight blank boxes in the formula," says the professor. "You have to fill each box with a number from 1 to 8, but you can only use each number once."

Of course this is simple so you plonk a few numbers in and have a quick go:

$$(4+3) \times (2-1) - (7+5) \div 8 + 6 = ?$$

Here's a chance to show off one of your tricks! You can impress everybody by working out the bits in the right order as we found out a few pages ago in the "brackets" section. First you zip through the numbers in the brackets and get

$$7 \times 1 - 12 \div 8 + 6 = ?$$

Next it's time for multiplying and dividing:

$$7 - 1\tfrac{1}{2} + 6 = ?$$

And finally you do the last bit of adding and subtracting to get an answer of $11\frac{1}{2}$. All too easy, isn't it?

"So you got your sums right," sneers the professor, "but what a feeble little answer! When I put the numbers in, my answer was $76\frac{4}{5}$. You'll never beat that!"

So that's the way he wants to play it, eh? Of course you're not going to ignore a challenge like this. Can you find a way of filling the numbers 1–8 into the formula and getting an answer bigger than the professor's?

A devious duel!

You could use the Fiendish Formula to challenge one or more friends.

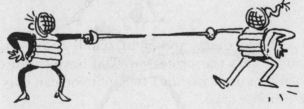

What you need:
- The forty number cards from a pack of playing cards.
- A sheet of paper with a copy of the formula (with the blank spaces) for each player.

How to play:
- Shuffle the cards and put them face down.
- Take turns to turn over one card from the pile.
- Every time you turn over a card, choose one of your blank boxes to write in the number on the

card. (You cannot change the position of a number once you have written it in!)

- When all of you have filled up your fiendish formulae it's time to work them out.
- Whoever's formula turns out to have the highest value wins!

(Of course, the trick of this game is to know which boxes need to have high numbers, and which boxes need to have low numbers!)

OH NO! LOOK...

...we've reached the end of the book!

Just as we're all ready to blast off into Murderous Maths hyperspace for some totally outrageous fun, we've run out of pages! Hopefully we'll all meet up again in another *Murderous Maths* book and see where it takes us, but in the meantime thanks for coming along this far and let's face it, we have come a long way together. Not only have we picked up some clever stuff, we've also had some laughs. We've found out how big a hairy clumpette is and above all we've learnt how to survive. Now that we're armed with the essential arithmetricks, we can face up to any ugly numbers that life throws our way and spit them right back with ribbons round them.

Of course there will always be one or two people who don't think that the arithmetricks are worth bothering with. You don't have to look hard to find them...

As for the rest of us, this book has come to a finish far too soon. Don't you just HATE it when you're just about to have a really good time, but then everything suddenly stops when you least expect it?

It's like you've just run a really deep bath, you've tipped in loads of your favourite bubble mixture...

...you've got a glass of pop with two straws and ice cubes to drink...

...your clean pants are warming up on the radiator...

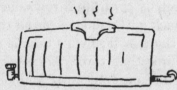

...and you've got a really exciting book all ready to read in which you're just getting to the good bit.

You close the door, throw your clothes off and put your leg over the side. Carefully you push your toe through the bubbles and down into the water which is just that tiny right amount too hot. Mmmm! Slowly you lower yourself in and sink back into the water. You pick up your book, avoiding the bubbles, and are about to let out a really satisfied sigh, when ...